Expert Systems and Fuzzy Systems

Expert Systems and Fuzzy Systems

Constantin Virgil Negoita

**Hunter College
City University of New York**

The Benjamin/Cummings Publishing Company, Inc.
Menlo Park, California • Reading, Massachusetts
London • Amsterdam • Don Mills, Ontario • Sydney

Sponsoring Editor: Alan Apt
Production Editor: Larry Olsen
Copy Editor: Antonio Padial
Text Designer: Nancy Benedict
Cover Designer: Gary Head

Library of Congress Cataloging in Publication Data

Negoiță, C. V. (Constantin Virgil)
  Expert systems and fuzzy systems.

  Bibliography: p.
  Includes index.
    1. Expert systems (Computer science)   2. Fuzzy
systems.   I. Title.
QA76.9.E96N44 1984   001.53'5   84-12324
ISBN 0-8053-6840-X

DEFGHIJ-HA-898765

The Benjamin/Cummings Publishing Company, Inc.
2727 Sand Hill Road
Menlo Park, California 94025

To
LOTFI ZADEH
the pioneer

Preface

How machines can be made smarter is a question that has confronted the computing field since its inception. Mere repetition of steps—for instance, adding numbers, inverting matrices, or even solving equations—presupposes hard-coded instructions. Any traditional computer program directs the machine to access data, but decisions about how to process those data are invariably hard-coded in the language of the program and stored in the memory during program execution. These decisions are made by the human programmer, who has the knowledge to make them.

Knowledge engineering is a discipline devoted to integrating human knowledge in computer systems. The distinctive characteristic of any knowledge-based system is that its processes are state-driven rather than hard-coded. Decisions about how to process data are part of the knowledge of the system. In other words, an intelligent system writes its program. Knowledge is procedural, in the sense that it tells how the data concerning a problem can be manipulated to solve it. By internalizing procedural knowledge as a model of the world, the machine becomes intelligent.

An expert system is an information system that can pose and answer questions relating to information borrowed from human experts and stored in the system's knowledge base. The fact that answers are automatically extracted from the data descriptions, by a user-invisible inference procedure, results in a great degree of data independence. Not only can users represent data in a high-level, human-oriented manner, but they are also spared the effort of describing the operations used to retrieve those data.

Because the knowledge base in an expert system is put there by human experts, and because much human knowledge is vague, it is usually true that facts and rules are neither totally certain nor totally consistent. For this reason, a basic issue in the design of expert systems is how to equip them with a computational capability for evidence transmission.

To solve this problem, researchers have augmented the inference procedures with mechanisms that combine evidence degrees according to the rules of plausible reasoning. *Plausible reasoning* is simply drawing conclusions from facts that seem to be correct. In most systems, this mechanism is purely heuristic. Recently, however, some investigators have tried to make that mechanism mathematically sound.

A promising approach is based on the theory of fuzzy sets. In this case, we speak about *approximate reasoning*, which means drawing conclusions by taking the consistency of the facts into account. The treatment of fuzziness is a critical issue in knowledge representation. To say that a word is fuzzy is to say that sometimes there is no definite answer as to whether or not the word applies to something. The indeterminacy is due to an aspect of the meaning of the word rather than to the state of our knowledge. In all expert systems based on symbolic manipulation and plausible reasoning, uncertainty is supposed to reside in the state of our knowledge. In expert systems based on semantic manipulation and approximate reasoning, the emphasis is on fuzziness viewed as an intrinsic property of natural language.

An evident advantage of the fuzzy set approach is the possibility of representing numeric and linguistic variables in a uniform way and of using a sound formalism to handle them.

If we represent facts as objects and rules as morphisms, the mathematical theory of categories is a good language for describing the mechanisms of evidence combination. The difference between plausible and approximate reasoning becomes the difference between the categories on which we model the facts. In this way, an algebra of knowledge becomes available to the system designer, and knowledge diagrams become models of both production systems or declarative systems used in logic programming.

In this book, I attempt to bring together the fundamentals of approximate reasoning and to illustrate the concepts with examples wherever possible. I have tried to present the role of fuzzy systems in knowledge engineering so that it is accessible to a wide audience, including those interested in the philosophy and logic of such systems as well as those interested in their design and application. For this reason, this book is introductory, and certain simplifications have been made to ease an understanding of the most important features of knowledge-based computing. Because in real computing fuzzy sets are tables, I preferred to present them as such. For each chapter, extensive annotated Readings have been included. Although this is a textbook, it does not include sample problems to solve. The annotated Readings pose sufficient real problems, and it seemed inappropriate to add contrived ones. The reader is warned that real expert systems are tailor-made.

This attempt to provide the new or experienced knowledge engineer with a survey of the most important material on the subject necessarily leaves some gaps. I have restricted myself somewhat to management-oriented applications, in which facts and rules are ill-defined and only a semantic approach seems to succeed. Perhaps the strongest implication of this approach is that it casts knowledge engineers in a new role. The problem-solving power of an expert system based on plausible reasoning and symbolic manipulation is primarily a function of the domain-specific information in the knowledge base and is only secondarily a function of the system's inference method. The problem-solving power of an expert system based on approximate reasoning and semantic manipulation is primarily a function of the inference method it employs. No longer are knowledge engineers merely intermediaries between the human expert and the developing knowledge base. In their new role, they are independent of both.

This observation deserves an explanation. Knowledge acquisition has been a long-standing bottleneck in artificial intelligence. Certainly, the most powerful knowledge systems are those that contain the most knowledge. Symbolic systems deal with description assertion and encoding of decision rules. Emphasis is on recursion and list structures, which can be treated by procedural languages.

Knowledge systems based on approximate reasoning are oriented less toward list structures and more toward logic programming. In this case, programming style bears little resemblance to the style of procedural languages, such as PL/1, Pascal, or even LISP. A conventional flowchart is of no help to those writing a logic program. The programmer must concentrate instead on the meaning of what is to be achieved, and he must express that meaning in a declarative style.

A major issue in this approach is the use of natural language and syntax. Making software user friendly will become progressively more critical in the next decade, as more powerful machines become available to a wider range of individuals than ever before. Many computer users will have little computer science training or inclination to get the training. They will want to use natural language in any dialogue with any computer. Only the fuzzy system approach makes such communication possible.

According to this book, a semantic system is software that uses fuzzy set technology to translate the meaning of a vocabulary. Once the knowledge engineer has developed the semantic system, the user can exploit it without any interface. With a semantic system, the user can encode knowledge in many forms: production rules, production systems, and verbal models. A verbal model can be viewed as a production system with mathematical operators. This book emphasizes the advantage of this approach to a semantic system: production systems can be treated as decision tables, and dynamic models can be treated with linguistic variables.

This is the kind of expertise used in management, and I hope that readers will see how knowledge systems can become a practical reality in decision making. If knowledge systems are developed responsibly, the result will be a significant improvement in both human systems management and human management systems.

C. V. Negoita

Contents

CHAPTER FOUR

Knowledge Representation   69

CHAPTER FIVE

Approximate Reasoning   95

CHAPTER SIX

Knowledge Engineering in Decision Support Systems   117

CHAPTER SEVEN

Knowledge Engineering in Management Expert Systems   141

APPENDIX

The Categorial Analysis of Logic   165

Expert Systems and Fuzzy Systems

CHAPTER ONE

Introduction

EXPERT COMPUTER SYSTEMS

When historians rank the technology of the present century, expert systems will almost certainly be high on the list. Expert systems—software systems that mimic the deductive or inductive reasoning of a human expert—belong to the family of information-intensive machines. For a task to qualify for knowledge engineering, there must be at least one acknowledged human expert.

The primary use of expert systems thus far has been in capital-intensive areas, such as oil drilling or exploration, where human experts are scarce and the cost of equipment lying idle is so high that the price of an expert system can be recaptured rapidly. Expert systems gained early success in medicine because a great deal of effort was spent writing down the best-known ways to solve problems. Indeed, some expert systems diagnose disease as well as the average medical practitioner does. Similarly, finance and accounting early lent themselves to expert systems, because knowledge in those areas is concrete and can be incorporated into a knowledge base relatively easily. In many fields, however, expertise is ill-defined and can be represented in an expert system only by special means.

The coming decade will to be devoted to magnifying human mental power by changing the basic design of computers so that they can carry on intelligent, natural intercourse with humans.

People speak "natural" languages, such as English or French. Computers speak "unnatural" languages, such as Pascal, FORTRAN, or BASIC. Large-scale expert systems depend on natural language as front ends to knowledge bases.

Production Systems

Expert systems require two things: a collection of facts and rules about a given field and a way of making inferences from those facts and rules. Any rule is a pattern-invoked program. Such a program is not called by other programs in the ordinary way but is instead activated whenever certain conditions hold in the data.

One pattern-invoked program of particular interest is the production rule

condition IMPLIES action

The condition is usually one or more predicates that test properties of the current state of facts. The action in turn changes the current state of the facts. Rules are frequently formulated in natural language, whose precision or vagueness reflects the human expert's knowledge. For instance, the production rule

price is low IMPLIES profit should be below normal

can be used individually or in a production system.

A production system consists primarily of a set of condition-action rules and operates in cycles. During each cycle, the conditions of each production rule are matched against the current state of facts. When rules and conditions match, actions are taken. Those actions affect the current state of facts, making new production rules match.

A promising feature of production systems is their modularity. Because each production rule is relatively independent of every other production rule, we could, in principle, construct modular systems. Production systems differ substantially from conventional computer programs because their tasks have no algorithmic solutions and because such systems must use incomplete information to make decisions.

Logic Programming

In any production rule, knowledge is procedural in the sense that it tells how the data for a problem can be manipulated to solve a problem. Procedural knowledge can also be represented by logic programming. In logic programming, one can express knowledge as either facts or rules. The basic building units of both facts and rules are predications, that is, expressions that say simple things about the individuals in a universe. For instance, the piece of knowledge "Peter likes Sarah" can be represented as

LIKES (Peter, Sarah, m)

Predications are represented by a predicate name followed by a list of arguments. An argument can be the name of an individual or a measure of degree.

Rules, by contrast, have the general form

$$P_1 \text{ if } (P_2 \text{ and } P_3 \text{ and } \dots \text{ and } P_n)$$

where P_i stands for predications. For example, the general rule that Peter and Sarah are friends can be stated as

FRIENDS (Peter, Sarah) if LIKES (Peter, Sarah) and
LIKES (Sarah, Peter)

If all the conditions hold, then the conclusion holds.

Once a set of facts and rules has been defined, one can deduce information from those facts and rules. This deduction is done by writing a query, an expression of form

$$P_2 \text{ and } P_3 \text{ and } \dots \text{ and } P_n?$$

For instance, given the world description

(1) LIKES (x, y)
(2) TALL (x)
(3) PERSON (x, y, z)

one can write the query

WHO LIKES A TALL PERSON?

Inference takes place automatically. The fact that answers are automatically extracted from the data descriptions by a user-invisible procedure results in a great degree of data independence. Not only can users represent data in a high-level, human-oriented manner (rather than in terms of bits, arrays, etc.), but they are also free from the effort of describing the operations used to retrieve the data. These operations are implicit in the inference mechanisms, which give an operational meaning to the purely descriptive fact and rule used.

Intelligence Means Internalization

Interest in the foundations of expert systems was sparked by difficulties encountered with evidence combination. Efforts to understand, formulate, and resolve the problems of inference led to some questions about the definition of artificial intelligence. Can a machine be intelligent? After all, what is intelligence? According to the expert system theorists, intelligence means the internalization of a model of the external milieu. The computer culture defined intelligence as an intentional movement.

Up to that point, intelligence had been a concern of the soft sciences. When it became a concern of the hard sciences, ontology entered the modern world. Some modern philosophers, speaking about being, define it as fulfilled in an intentional movement. They say that being possesses no more than a potentiality for its own realization. Thus, contemporary ontologists favor dynamic potentiality as the definition of being.*

Once nature is directed toward its proper end, say the philosophers, it finds fixity in an opening. A closure made for an opening is, for example, the closure of rules and its opening in language. This is the case for every external milieu that can be internalized. According to the same philosophers, to grow in being means to transform external milieux into internal ones. For humans, being is evidently the striving for and possibility of reintegration in another modality. Culture, for instance, which at the beginning represents a perfect external milieu, becomes at the end an internal milieu for those fulfilled in it. In fact, spiritual life is this movement from the external to the internal. The topic does not belong to modern ontology alone. In a much older formulation, it belongs to those theologians who said that, after the Fall, Grace acts on man from the outside.

Systems theory can formalize this perspective, and cybernetics can project it on organized reality. Cybernetics is the science of communications in and control of machines and animals. If one applies the principles of cybernetics to labor-saving machines and methods, the result is automation. A relatively long time ago, automation, with its emphasis on regulators, brought the internal model principle to the fore. According to this principle, a control system needs feedback and must incorporate in the feedback loop a suitable model of the dynamic structure of the exogenous variables. In plain English, before acting, one has to know the environment. Again, the conclusion is very old: rational means known beforehand.

Philosophers and cyberneticians are in total agreement when they link intelligence with knowledge. Lately, mathematicians have come to the same conclusion. Studying abstract structures and trying to generalize the category of sets, they focused on an intelligent structure and called it *topos* (place) because it internalized its logic. The expert system approach is a step in this direction. When knowledge is internalized, the machine becomes "beinglike" or "rationallike."

---

* C. Noica, "Becoming into Being," *Ed.S.E.Buc.*, 1981 (reviewed in *Kybernetes* 11 (1982): 147).

Pullback Versus Feedback

Both control theory and knowledge engineering are dominated by the internal model principle, but the difference between them is substantial. In control theory, the intelligent regulator is external to the regulated system. In knowledge engineering, the self-regulated system is intelligent. An intelligent machine is free, if freedom is defined as the possibility to act according to internalized goals. Any artificial intelligence approach, viewed from the internalization perspective, builds a disequilibrium of sequential changes, now and then exhibiting quasi-equilibria on the way.

The fundamental question is "What laws govern rationality?" Any answer emphasizes the realization of a goal. In conventional programming, the program is a series of steps controlling the machine and minimizing the distance between an actual state and a desired one. The desired state is a reference, outside the machine. We use the term *feedback* to mean that the system is controlled by the margin of error with reference to an external goal. In expert systems, the desired goal is internalized in the knowledge base, and the machine achieves the goal by resorting to (pulling back in) the structure of facts. *Pullback* means a movement governed by an internal goal. We say that the behavior of the system is controlled by pullback.

The principle of pullback is a direct consequence of any knowledge representation based on logic, whether that logic is two-valued or multivalued. Pullback is best explained when the knowledge base is modeled as a category. One goal of this book is to discuss this problem in more detail.

The Computer Revolution

Some specialists question that expert systems represent a quantum leap from conventional computer systems. They argue that expert systems represent an evolutionary rather than a revolutionary development. Computers and information systems are well-structured environments for accomplishing a task. Expert systems do something similar: they are a record of accumulated experience. The programs lead users in a logical way through alternatives that, without computers, they would have to recognize themselves. Combining in one computer program the know-how to solve a problem and accumulated data and experience is a major step forward, but no new knowledge is being created. Know-how is not knowledge, and training is not education, no matter how important know-how and training are.

From a social perspective, expert systems have much in common with mathematical models, and the credibility of both has often been questioned. If modeling computers are used by unsophisticated technical workers, intellectual insight is gained at the expense of intuition. Expert systems allow organizations to place unsophisticated staff in key analytical positions. Working knowledge does not come easily from an algorithm that is used uncritically under varying conditions. It is vital to understand the roles computing is coming to play. It is also vital not to overstate the contributions of otherwise interesting technologies. Improved literacy does not depend on better computers, and computer-based systems do not always yield better decisions. In some places, people have no access to an average practitioner, and some specialists argue that an artificial expert is better than none at all. A sure fact is that work on languages and systems for knowledge representation will significantly reduce the effort required to develop intelligent systems. These systems, in turn, will help users to focus more on the problem itself than on the implementation of the underlying program.

Expert systems evolved from machines dedicated to numeric computation. What is new is that they assess the meaning of information and understand the problem to be solved. Intelligent programming software will allow machines to take over the burden of programming, and this is a revolution.

THE FIELD AND THE BOOK

An expert system is a machine that makes inferences from internalized facts and rules. The facts and the rules are chunks of knowledge or statements about the external world. Yet, it is a well-known fact that any observer's ability to make precise but significantly certain statements about complex external worlds decreases as their complexity increases. Precision and certainty seem to be incompatible.

In the philosophy of science, this fact has been known for a long time. In the sixth century, Leontius from Byzantium observed: "Our impression of the world is general but vague, not revealing the truth; and if we attempt to particularize by division into genera and species and individuals, the general view is lost: we are heading not towards the truth but towards an infinite regress.* Fourteen centuries later, Pierre Duhem distinguished between practical facts expressed in vague, qualitative, ordinary language and theoretical facts expressed in pre-

---

* A. Armstrong, *The Cambridge History of Later Greek and Early Medieval Philosophy,* (Cambridge University Press, 1970) p. 490.

cise, quantitative language.* Duhem argued that confidence in the truth of a vague assertion may be justified just because of its vagueness, which makes the assertion compatible with a whole range of observed facts. The laws of physics acquire detailed precision at the expense of the fixed and absolute certainty of common-sense laws. According to Duhem, there is a balance between precision and certainty; one is increased only to the detriment of the other.

This principle explains the considerable intellectual investment required to approximate reasoning. The key idea is the representation of a fact as an evaluation and of a rule as a transformation of evaluations. Such an evaluation is a function, as is the fuzzy set. The exact relationship of a fuzzy set to an ordinary set is best perceived by recalling the definition of the characteristic function of a set. The characteristic function of an ordinary set has this form:

$$U \rightarrow \{0,1\}$$

This set maps the universe U to a set of two elements. This is a binary choice between being in or out of the set.

A fuzzy set is a function with more than two values, usually with values in the unit interval

$$U \rightarrow [0,1]$$

This function allows a continuum of possible choices. Such a function can be used to describe imprecise terms. For example, the term *old* can be defined according to the universe of human ages. Clearly, someone over seventy is old, so the degree of membership of an age seventy or greater is 1.0. It is not as certain that a sixty-year-old is old. Rather than saying that a sixty-year-old is old or not, one can say that that individual is partially old. We could evaluate the degree of oldness at age sixty as 0.7. In this way, the vagueness of the term *old* can be captured mathematically and dealt with in an algorithmic fashion.

As in ordinary set theory, the characteristic function of fuzzy sets links fuzzy set theory with logic. The degree of membership corresponds to a truth value of the statement "is a member of," which is equivalent to "is partially defined as." This correspondence has a profound implication for artificial reasoning.

Reasoning means drawing conclusions from facts. When the facts are represented as setlike objects, the meaning of the logical operators AND, OR is precisely defined by the category of these objects. The logic

* Pierre Duhem, *La théorie physique: Son objet et sa structure* (Paris: Chevalier & Rivière, 1906).

of approximate reasoning is internalized in the category of generalized sets.

Fuzzy sets can be seen as states of fuzzy systems. The dynamics of a fuzzy system is a movement in the structure of fuzzy sets. Universal constructions in the category of fuzzy sets can be exploited to model the processes taking place in a knowledge base precisely because a knowledge base can be modeled as a category. In this way, we can speak about knowledge diagrams and about an algebra of approximate reasoning.

In 1965, Zadeh introduced the concept of a fuzzy set as a model of a vague fact. Soon after, three important events took place.

First, Duhem's principle of incompatibility was explained by the category of fuzzy sets. It was observed that one can model a synthesis by a pullback in this structure. In this way, one can explain the need for abstraction as a need for structural stability. Taking into account that the category of fuzzy sets is equivalent to the category of concepts, one can explain how the search for certainty leads to a loss of precision. This is how humans cope with complexity.

Second, this theory was confirmed by so-called qualitative analysis with linguistic values. Qualitative analysis was a new tool for the system analyst. For the first time, simulation of verbal models seemed possible. Verbal models have variables whose values are not numbers but words. Quantitative techniques could now be applied to qualitative problems. The great advantage of quantitative models is their built-in capability to provide consistent deductions of consequences. For example, quantitative analysis has proved an indispensable tool in physics because its variables are arithmomorphic; that is, they have numeric values. Fuzzy mathematics made it possible to use verbal models exactly as mathematical models are used in physics. An old barrier was eliminated, and linguistic models—which dominate the social sciences and heuristic knowledge in general—can now be handled by computers.

Third, knowledge engineers began working with human experts and painstakingly building knowledge bases. In this task, they met with imprecision in facts and lines of reasoning. Although there has been intermittent communication between knowledge engineering and the theory of fuzzy systems, the two disciplines have evolved along parallel but largely independent paths.

The main path of knowledge engineering has been attention to *symbolic manipulation* and especially to systems that draw on large production rules bases. These systems discover lines of reasoning leading to solutions to symbolically stated problems. The number of real-world applications of such systems is growing rapidly. The discipline of knowledge engineering has emerged from the proliferation of expert systems. The goal of this discipline is to plan, design, construct, and manage expert systems for the transfer, utilization, and extension of knowledge, including inexact and subjective knowledge.

The path of fuzzy systems has been characterized by attention to *semantic manipulations*. Imprecision in lines of reasoning was considered to be the result of imprecision in the definitions of words. Because imprecision resides in language, it is therefore introduced arbitrarily from outside the system.

This text describes such semantic manipulations and gives the reader the mathematical background necessary to understand the algorithms used in approximate reasoning. With this background, and with the knowledge that practical results have demonstrated the reasonableness of this approach, the reader can begin to use algorithms in decision support systems knowledgeably.

Expert Systems as Decision Support Systems

A decision support system can be defined as an interactive computer system that directly helps executives make decisions. Because of its information-processing speed, a decision support system has the potential to be part of an effective man–machine problem-solving system.

Decision support systems are most effective in solving *semistructured* problems, that is, problems with sufficient structure to make computer and analytical aids valuable, but problems in which human judgment is still essential.

There are two basic types of decision systems: procedural and definitional. In procedural systems, one commands the computer to do each step. Definitional systems are problem-oriented systems. They are sometimes called nonprocedural, to distinguish them from procedural systems. In procedural systems, one uses the machine not as an intelligent being that is trying to help but rather as a tool that adopts a predetermined solution scheme and follows a detached list of instructions very rapidly. Users of nonprocedural systems do not try to figure out how to solve the problem; rather, they rely on the computer to read and in some sense understand the problem as an expert might.

Since the early 1960s, there have been attempts to use computers to address managerial problems. Later in the decade, operations research and management scientists began to promote mathematical modeling and simulation in decision making, but management information systems suffered from the major defect that they could be applied only with the aid of technical staff. Because of the difficulty of communicating with technical staff, managers and their support groups were usually isolated from the problem-solving tools. Executives needed direct access and a personal dialogue with computer-based tools. A major shift in this direction began in about 1969, when the first of the financial planning languages appeared on the market.

A good example is REVEAL, a decision support system produced by Decision Products Services, Inc. This was the first system to include approximate reasoning based on fuzzy sets in a planning model. This significant innovation is designed to allow models that use judgment and professional expertise in conjunction with the standard arithmetic operations used in planning.

The new and creative movement of decision support systems began to evolve from the conceptual base underlying a few of these languages. The idea is to provide direct support to managers and their staffs without the direct assistance of programmers. Decision support systems are now a reality, but the movement goes further: management information systems must become intelligent management systems.

This text describes some intelligent management systems based on semantic manipulations allowed by approximate reasoning. REVEAL is used here for its simple, elegant, and efficient policy routines that describe information in and retrieve it from data bases. A data base can be interrogated with a query of the form

$$P_1 \text{ and } P_2 \text{ and } \ldots \text{ and } P_n$$

where the policy routines P_i are predications in natural language. Answers are extracted automatically from the data bases by a user-invisible inference procedure. Not only are users allowed to formulate a query in natural language, but they also need not describe the operations used for retrieval.

This is a typical case of fuzzy optimization, multicriteria decision making in which constraints are formulated as fuzzy sets. Any fuzzy optimization problem is a movement in the structure of predications toward a synthesis. Finding "the best" solution means finding a particular fuzzy set in this structure.

User-invisible inferences are permitted by special constructions in the category of fuzzy sets when the system formulates the policy routines, production rules, or descriptions for logic programming. The laws of this category allow this inference by the system. The inference mechanism is a consequence of the methodology adopted for knowledge representation. In semantic systems, reasoning is derived from representation.

To understand approximate reasoning, one must understand the basic ideas for organizing knowledge according to the laws of the category of fuzzy sets. In Chapters Two through Seven, I define and explain these basic ideas.

Chapter Two, Exact and Inexact Reasoning in Knowledge Engineering, is a discussion of why inexact reasoning is important and what can be learned from analyzing it. Although one can study this problem at a mathematically sophisticated level, it is also possible to gain a great deal of useful insight at a more introductory and expository level. At this more elementary level, plausible reasoning is determined by observation, and approximate reasoning is determined by evaluation. To turn from observation to representation means to recognize things by similarities instead of by differences.

In everyday life, we often deal with imprecisely defined properties or quantities: "a few books," "a long story," "a beautiful woman," "a tall man." In the mid-1960s, Zadeh introduced the notion of fuzzy set to allow such concepts to be modeled. It is not immediately obvious how to construct a foundation of fuzzy sets. Some texts present fuzzy sets as sets of ordered pairs. These texts give the impression of distinguishing between a fuzzy set and its membership function, which is an assignment of truth values in the unit interval. Any appearance of lack of rigor is easily dispelled by defining the fuzzy set as a function. This definition makes evident the possibility of replacing the unit interval with some general structure. These ideas are discussed further in Chapter Three, Fuzzy Sets.

Much of the knowledge internalized in a knowledge base can be represented as production rules, which are IF-THEN relations. In real life, relationships as well as properties can be imprecise—"similar to," "a friend of," "to the left of," "near," and so on. We can handle such relations exactly as we handle fuzzy sets: we simply define a fuzzy relation on a set as a fuzzy subset of the Cartesian product. This subject is discussed in Chapter Four, Knowledge Representation.

Once representation is understood, the rules of inference emerge. When a question is asked of the knowledge base, a knowledge tree is generated. The derivation of the knowledge tree is a forward process, whereas the evaluation of the tree is a backward contraction process— a pullback in the structure of facts. Perhaps the most interesting consequence of an algebraic approach to the theory of knowledge trees is the fact that truth questions (Is John tall?), value questions (How is John?), and variable questions (Who is tall?) can be explained by the same mechanism: the knowledge diagram. These ideas are discussed in Chapter Five, Approximate Reasoning.

Whatever the modeling value of a fuzzy set may be, it is of considerable interest to workers in decision science. Chapter Six, Knowledge Engineering in Decision Support Systems, describes some ways fuzzy sets are used in qualitative information retrieval and in fuzzy optimization. Good applications make any science more exciting, and many management scientists welcomed the use of fuzzy numbers. There is support for the position that fuzzy optimization is knowledge engineering.

Chapter Seven concerns Knowledge Engineering in Management Expert Systems. If we accept that semantic manipulations are knowledge engineering, we see how to answer such difficult questions as "which is the best?" "what is coming?" and "what is going on?" Separating the semantic base of the knowledge system, we discover that we can use it independently in advisory systems or in knowledge amplifiers.

HISTORICAL SURVEY

The development of knowledge engineering and fuzzy systems is described in many good surveys. In this section, I attempt to trace how these developments merged into our present state of knowledge. My interest in knowledge engineering began in 1965 when I was preparing a Ph.D. thesis on information retrieval. In information retrieval, one uses natural language for content description and a strategy for searching. When indexing a book, for example, one represents the content by a set of words, called descriptors, that help determine which topics to retrieve.

To *retrieve* means to specify descriptors and to use rules for combining them in a sequence that conveys meaning. The skill with which these descriptors are used determines the effectiveness of the retrieval. In 1965, the criteria for how to search were based on a controlled list of allowable descriptors. Computer technologists have explored many different approaches to the problem of providing models of indexing. It would be tedious and unrewarding to describe them all. It is enough to say that all are based on the relation "the item x has the descriptor y." For instance, "John is tall" means that the item "John" has the descriptor "tall."

The relation between items and descriptors can be represented by a matrix. For example, the columns of the matrix can represent a vocabulary of descriptors, and the rows can represent the items indexed in a retrieval system. To enter an item into the system, one assigns descriptors to the item by tagging it with appropriate values. This assignment is indicated in each cell of the matrix. For example

	Tall	Intelligent	Famous
John	1	1	0
Mary	0	1	1
Peter	1	0	1

is such a matrix in which items are represented by subsets of descriptors.

If one is sure that the item x has the descriptor y, then values in the unit interval can replace 0 and 1, as in the matrix

	Tall	Intelligent	Famous
John	0.9	0.8	0
Mary	0.1	0.7	0.9
Peter	0.8	0.2	1

One cell in this matrix, for instance, means "John is tall is true to the degree 0.9."

This representation can be modeled as an associative triple, as follows

(item, descriptor, value)

Boolean or non-Boolean keyword retrieval systems operate at a symbolic level and therefore ignore much available semantic or contextual information. One way to overcome this is to model the meaning of the descriptor and to aggregate separate meanings.

In 1966, I was almost sure that the idea of a fuzzy set could be very fruitful. Instead of the triple

(John, tall, 0.9)

one can use the couple

(John IS tall)

and a description of "tall" given by the function

tall: heights $\rightarrow$ [0,1]

As I remember those days, I realize how fuzzy beginnings are. One stumbles through unknown regions, is led astray by analogies, is overwhelmed by new possibilities, and knows afterward what one should have known before. The second generation has the advantage of a picture that is clearer, if still incomplete. Certain landmarks on the fuzzy frontier of the essential have grown familiar. Forewarned and forearmed, those in the second generation can spot the most distant connections, unravel problems and give a coherent account of the whole field of study.

In 1970, I published my Ph.D. thesis, which set forth a fuzzy set approach to information retrieval centered on three basic elements: descriptors, morphisms, and goals. Morphisms permit us to move from descriptors to their synthesis. I described a knowledge item in terms of existing descriptors, and a query as a goal. I characterized the systems approach to information retrieval by a series of morphisms that successively move the initial state to the goal state.

A descriptor is a set of information items that can be viewed as an object in the category of sets. A synthesis of descriptors is a construction in this category, and two-valued logic is a consequence of adopting the model of sets. If the descriptor is modeled as a fuzzy set, we move from the category of sets to a new category characterized by new logic. The key problem of any information retrieval system based on fuzzy set technology centers on the logic operators used in combining evidence when individual descriptors are characterized by degrees of membership. Any serious approach to logic is categorial.

In 1972, I published my experiments at Atlas Computer Laboratory in England. Coping with fuzziness was a real problem, and, in Bucharest in 1973, I started a series of weekly discussions devoted to fuzzy systems.

The participants were mostly young scientists at the Institute of Management and Informatics, and the conversation was lively and unrestrained. Dan Ralescu, one of my first collaborators, was a regular participant. For two years, we shared the conviction that a fuzzy mathematics could and should be developed. One of our first papers was "Fuzzy Sets in Artificial Intelligence," and together we wrote a monograph whose English version was published simultaneously in 1975 by Birkhauser Verlag in Switzerland and Halsted Press in New York.

The central idea of this book was the representation theorem: any fuzzy set is a family of crisp sets. The category of fuzzy sets is, therefore, equivalent to the category of families of level sets, and the fuzzy set is a model of a setlike object, the generalized set.

In the summer of 1976, I met Paul Flondor, Mircea Sularia, and Corneliu Stefanescu, who came to work with me in fuzzy optimization. At that time, I was already aware of the essential unity of the problems of both information retrieval and fuzzy optimization as defined by Bellman and Zadeh. The descriptors in information retrieval and the constraints in fuzzy optimization must be treated alike. In both cases the evaluation process is a backward contraction into the category of facts. Our investigations took three directions: the application of the representation theorem in fuzzy programming, the embedding of the theory of fuzzy sets in topoi, and the study of the backtracking contraction process.

At the same time, Zadeh's superb idea of compositional inference made it possible to speak about virtual descriptors in information retrieval. The idea of a rule supplementing the idea of a descriptor opened the door for expert systems. The system has direct, manipulatory access to knowledge, as opposed to having the knowledge built-in. What follows is the subject of this book.

In 1983, in a seminar at the Department of Computer Science at Hunter College in New York, I examined a number of specific question-answering systems based on approximate reasoning. A phenomenon occurred repeatedly: the pullback construction from the category of fuzzy sets. Those events gave me the motivation to write this book.

READINGS

Winston, P. H. 1975. *Artificial intelligence.* Reading, Mass.: Addison-Wesley.

This classic, widely read book on artificial intelligence unfortunately treated problems so well that it gave the impression that all problems were solved. It says that the central goals of artificial intelligence are to make computers more useful and to understand the principles that make intelligence possible. It says also that wanting to make computers *be* intelligent is not the same as wanting to make computers *simulate.* There is neither an obsession with mimicking human intelligence nor a prejudice against using methods of machine intelligence. The overall result is a new point of view and a new methodology, which lead to new theories.

Barr, A., and Feigenbaum, E., eds. 1982. *The handbook of artificial intelligence.* Los Altos, Ca.: Kaufmann.

This state-of-the art, long, important book traces the evolution of expert systems. The reader will find that artificial intelligence research in the 1960s identified and explored several general-purpose problem-solving techniques, and this work introduced and refined the concept of heuristic research. Later it became clear that although heuristic-search management is still a major concern in the construction of any expert system, efficient implementation and automated maintenance of large knowledge bases must also be addressed. A particularly important design issue is devising effective means for acquiring large amounts of knowledge from the human experts, who insist on "talking about" what they do rather than "dumping" what they know, as computers do. The issue of acquiring knowledge from human experts is now seen as a part of the general problem of *transfer of expertise.* Because humans are both the source and the users of expertise, current concerns in expert systems design center on how humans talk about what they know.

Specialists are distinguished from laypeople and general practitioners in a technical domain by their vast task-specific knowledge acquired from training, from subsequent reading, and especially from long experience. Whether they be car mechanics or neurosurgeons, experts can solve problems that others cannot because they have knowledge that nonexperts do not. Sometimes expertise means knowing specific facts that have been committed to memory over the years, and sometimes expertise means having hunches (making educated guesses) about how to solve a problem. Representing and using the various types of knowledge that characterize expertise constitute one principal focus in expert systems research. Among the things that an expert system needs to know are:

1. Facts about the domain: "The automatic choke on '77 Chevies often gets stuck on cold mornings."

2. Hard-and-fast rules of procedures: "New price should be lower than others' new price."

3. Problems and useful strategies for problems (heuristics): "If opposition prices are not very low, then our price must be competitive."

4. A "theory" of the domain: "Acute pyelonephritis usually presents heavy irritation, occasionally fever, and always some malaise."

Many of the knowledge representations that characterize human expertise are hunchlike, in the sense that they do not constitute definite consequences of actions or certainty of conclusions. Reasoning based on such knowledge was the key idea that made expert systems possible and is the main problem in developing their power further. In particular, *inexact reasoning*—using hunches or heuristics to guide and focus what would otherwise be a search of an impossibly large space—has resulted in systems with near-human problem-solving abilities. Indeed, these systems have at times proved superior to human experts.

Davis, R., and Lenat, D. 1982. *Knowledge-based systems in artificial intelligence.* New York: McGraw-Hill, Computer Science Series.

This book reports in detail on two major research efforts nurtured by the Stanford Heuristic Programming Project, whose primary focus over the past fifteen years has been the development and exploitation of the knowledge-base paradigm. In an introduction, Feigenbaum and Buchanan set the historical context for the two cases and discuss their significance.

The Stanford Project's first foray into clinical medicine was the MYCIN effort, a program that performed consultations with physicians about infectious disease diagnosis and antimicrobial therapy. Issues in knowledge acquisition and representation arose from this work and provided inspiration for Davis's work on TEIRESIAS, a collection of programs whose overall task is to assist a user of a complex program such as MYCIN to understand the reasoning chain and to find errors in the knowledge base. Lenat's computer program is called AM. It makes interesting and plausible conjectures about number theory. AM does not prove them; its task is to suggest them. Because the set of possible theorems is very big, AM needs considerable knowledge of mathematics to sort out the interesting ones.

Both the TEIRESIAS and AM programs are excellent examples of the *art* of knowledge engineering. These programs manipulate large knowledge bases and do not merely execute fixed instructions. The aim here is not simply to build a program that exhibits a certain behavior, but to use the program construction process itself as a way of explicating knowledge in the field. In fact, the program text is a medium of expression of many forms of knowledge about the task and its solution.

The AM program models one aspect of elementary mathematics research: it develops new concepts under the guidance of a large body of heuristic rules. Mathematics is considered a type of intelligent behavior, not merely a finished report. The local heuristics communicate, via an agenda mechanism, a global list of tasks for the system to perform, along with reasons why each task is plausible. A single task might direct AM to define a new concept, to explore some facet of an existing concept, or to examine empirical data for regularities. Repeatedly, the program selects from the agenda the task with the strongest support and then executes it. Each concept is an active structured knowledge module. A hundred very incomplete modules are initially provided, each one corresponding to an elementary set-theoretic concept. These modules constitute a finite but immense space that AM explores, guided by a corpus of 250 rules. AM extends its knowledge base, ultimately rediscovering hundreds of common concepts and theorems.

The reader may ask, "How many levels can AM ascend?" This is a fuzzy notion, but Lenat states that a new level is reached when a valuable new bunch of connected concepts are defined in terms of concepts at a lower level. This experimental fact confirms a theory of concepts represented as fuzzy sets. Further, the reader may ask "What possible applications can such a program have?" In a chapter devoted to "Future Implications of This Project," Lenat discusses uses for the AM system, uses for ideas on how to create such systems, and conclusions that can be drawn for mathematics and science. To mitigate the problems caused by all-or-nothing execution, Davis follows MYCIN, accepting an approximate measure on top of the production rules structure. Uncertainty is based on measures of belief, and thus models human cognitive processes rather than statistics. In recent years, many other attempts have been made to use fuzzy logic in production systems. Although Davis does not mention the fact, the concept of a fuzzy production rule provides a direct model of humanlike reasoning, ranging from crisp to very vague. The research reported in this book is prior to 1977, but the reader can find interesting results in Mamdani and Gaines, below.

Mamdani, E. H., and Gaines, B. R., eds. 1981. *Fuzzy reasoning and its application.* London: Academic Press.

This book is a collection of papers that previously appeared in the *International Journal of Man-Machine Studies*, which played a leading role during the past years in disseminating research in the field. Papers are discussed individually below.

Zadeh, L. A. "PRUF—A Meaning Representation Language for Natural Languages." This is the key paper in the book. PRUF is an acronym for Possibilistic Relational Universal Fuzzy. The paper presents a meaning representation language that departs in several important respects from conventional approaches to the theory of meaning. First, the basic assumption underlying PRUF is that the imprecision intrinsic in natural languages is, for the most part, possibilistic. Thus, a proposition such as "John is tall" translates in PRUF into a possibility distribution of the variable HEIGHT(John), which associates with each value of the variable a number in the unit interval representing the possibility that HEIGHT(John) could assume the value in question. More generally, a proposition translates into a procedure, which returns a possibility distribution representing its meaning. In this sense, possibility distribution replaces truth as a foundation for representing meaning in natural languages. Second, the logic underlying PRUF is not a two-valued or multivalued logic, but a fuzzy logic in which the truth values are linguistic, that is, are of the form *true, not true, very true, more or less true*, and so on, with each such truth value representing a fuzzy subset of the unit interval.

The truth value of a proposition is defined further as its compatibility with a reference proposition, so that given two propositions, one can compute the truth of one relative to the other. Third, the quantifiers in PRUF can be linguistic. Because of the cardinality of a fuzzy set, quantifiers are given a concrete interpretation, which makes it possible to translate into PRUF such propositions as "Many tall men are much taller than most men," "All tall women are blonde is not very true," and so on. The concept of semantic equivalence in PRUF provides a basis for question-answering and inference from fuzzy premises.

Goguen, J. A. "Concept Representation in Natural and Artificial Languages: Axioms, Extensions and Applications for Fuzzy Sets." This paper reports research related to mathematics, philosophy, computer science, and linguistics. It gives a system of axioms for relatively simple form of fuzzy set theory and uses these axioms to consider the accuracy of representing concepts in various ways by fuzzy sets. By-products of this approach include a number of new operations and laws for fuzzy sets, parallel to those for ordinary sets, and a demonstration that all the basic operations are intrinsically determined. In addition, the paper explores both hierarchical and algorithmic extension of fuzzy sets as well as applications to problems in natural language semantics and combinatorics. Finally, the paper returns to the problem of representing concepts and discusses some implications of artificial intelligence.

Wenstop, F. "Deductive Verbal Models of Organizations." This paper explores the idea that loosely defined simulation models of organizational behavior can yield more significant information than conventional, precisely defined ones. Natural language has been used for this purpose. The values of the variables can thus be linguistic rather than numeric, and causal relationships between the variables can be formulated verbally rather than mathematically. Wenstop presents generative grammar, which restricts the set of allowed linguistic values and relations in a model specification. Generative grammar makes it possible to use fuzzy set theory to formulate a semantic model of the words in the vocabulary. The semantic model can be used to infer future behavior of a verbal model, given its linguistically stated initial state. This process was greatly facilitated by implementing the semantic model in an APL workspace. It was thus possible to write linguistic values and relations directly on a terminal, using a syntax very close to that of natural language. The semantic model could then be activated automatically and respond with the linguistic values of output variables.

Gupta, M. M., and Sanchez, E., eds. 1982. *Approximate reasoning in decision analysis.* Amsterdam: North-Holland.

Some papers on expert systems and medical diagnosis in this collection deserve attention. "CADIAG-2: Computer Assisted Medical Diagnosis Using Fuzzy Sets" reports research at the University of Vienna, Austria. "Learning of Fuzzy Production Rules for Medical Diagnosis" presents the research at the University of Torino, Italy.

"SPHINX: An Interactive System for Medical Diagnosis Aids," and "Soft Deduction Rules in Medical Diagnosis Processes" summarize events at the Faculté de Medicine, Marseilles, France. "The Use of Fuzzy Set Theory in Electrocardiological Diagnosis" reports the research at the University of Ghent, Belgium. "Fuzzy Set Model for Computerized Diagnosis Systems in Traditional Chinese Medicine" presents the work done at the Academia Sinica. In a survey of medical diagnosis and fuzzy subsets, Klaus Peter Adlassnig of the University of Vienna discusses fuzzy set theory and its ability to define inexact medical entities. His conclusion is that approximate reasoning is perfectly suited for designing and developing computer-assisted diagnostic and treatment recommendation systems. This detailed survey shows the wide and deep interest of researchers the world over in finding a solid basis in fuzzy theory for representing medical knowledge.

The emphasis on medical applications in this book is perhaps explained by the fact that one editor, E. Sanchez, is very active in the field. But medical applications are not singular. In other papers— for instance, "A Rule-Based Inference with Fuzzy Sets for Structural Damage Assessment" and "Fuzzy Systems in Civil Engineering"— the development of expert systems is well anticipated. A paper entitled "Linguistic Description of Human Judgements in Expert Systems and in the 'Soft' Sciences" gives a psychologist's point of view of the difference between measurements performed in the "hard" sciences and judgments that form the basis for decisions in the "soft" sciences.

Those who remember Fred Wenstop's pioneering 1975 Ph.D. dissertation (University of California, Berkeley) on applications of linguistic variables in the analysis of organizations will find Pierro Bonissone's paper, "A Fuzzy Set Based Linguistic Approach," equally interesting. Bonissone's paper is based on another Ph.D. dissertation and substantially develops the idea of linguistic approximation, a vital part of any semantic system.

Yager, R., ed. 1982. *Fuzzy set and possibility theory.* New York: Pergamon Press.

This contributed volume, based on a symposium on fuzzy sets held in 1981 in Acapulco, Mexico, emphasizes the importance of fuzzy logic in approximate reasoning. J. F. Baldwin's "An Automated Fuzzy Reasoning Algorithm" and C. J. Ernst's "An Approach to Management Expert Systems Using Fuzzy Logic" are must reading for those interested in knowing the potential utility of fuzzy logic in enforcing semantics and pragmatics of expert systems.

Kandel, A. 1982. *Fuzzy techniques in pattern recognition.* New York: Wiley.

This book has a bibliography of 3000 items, an indispensable study instrument for those interested in fuzzy systems and approximate reasoning.

CHAPTER TWO

Exact and Inexact Reasoning in Knowledge Engineering

A variety of methods have been used to construct expert systems in the past. In this chapter, we examine briefly but critically some of these methods in terms of the two components that define any knowledge-based system: its knowledge base and its inference mechanism.

Many researchers have used conventional programming techniques to design expert systems. These systems are typically implemented with contemporary procedural languages, and thus the knowledge of the system is represented by the statements of the underlying program. Inferences are generated simply by executing the statements in the program. In these systems, there is no clear-cut separation between the knowledge base and the inference mechanism: the two parts are inseparably interwoven.

Partly because of the limitations of this conventional approach, researchers in artificial intelligence have become interested in internalizing the knowledge base of an expert system. The "reasoning" of such a system is transparent; that is, it is able to justify its decisions. In this way, the system at times models human decision making.

One widely adopted approach to artificial intelligence has been the production rule, or implication. In production systems, associative knowledge is represented as a domain-specific set of conditional rules. Each rule has one of three forms. The first form is

$$antecedents \rightarrow consequences$$

The following rule is an example.

$$IF\ x\ is\ a\ dog\ THEN\ x\ is\ an\ animal.$$

A second form is

$$premise \rightarrow conclusion$$

This rule is an example of the second form:

IF stain is gram-positive THEN organism is *Streptococcus.*

A third form is

$$\text{situation} \rightarrow \text{action}$$

This rule is an example of the third form:

IF temperature is greater than 55°F THEN turn off boiler

In such sets of conditional rules, if certain conditions are true, then the conclusions are also true.

The inference mechanism in a production system is deductive; it is a rule interpreter that applies the rules in the knowledge base to particular cases. At any point in the problem-solving process, the rule interpreter must select which rules to evaluate. The inference mechanism can be antecedent driven or consequent driven. In an antecedent-driven system, the occurrence of an antecedent triggers a rule to infer its consequence. In a consequent-driven system, the interpreter, to establish a certain fact, selects a rule with that fact as a consequent and then tries to verify it by confirming that the antecedents are present.

A rather simple control structure assumes that the system has the overall goal of confirming or discarding hypotheses on the basis of the facts introduced by users. The main difficulty of this mechanism is its inability to cope with competing hypotheses. In other words, at the end of the deductive process a hypothesis is either true or false, thus depriving the user of an evaluation of the evidence.

To overcome this difficulty, the production rules have been augmented by an assignment mechanism, so called because it combines the evidence degrees of the input facts to obtain the degree of evidence assigned to a given hypothesis. In most mechanisms, this assignment is purely empirical. Some recent investigation, however, has focused on making such an assignment mechanism mathematically sound.

A brief review of the best-known approaches for dealing with uncertainty in facts and implication in expert systems follows. In this chapter, only three methods for handling uncertainty in expert systems are considered in detail. They are the subjective probabilities method used in PROSPECTOR (Ishizuka, Fu, and Yao, 1982 a and b), the confirmation theory used in MYCIN (Shortliffe and Buchanan, 1975), and Shafer's theory of evidence (Dempster, 1967; Shafer, 1976).

Finally, approximate reasoning is presented as a totally different point of view. Some comments about subjective and objective evaluations clarify the origin of fuzziness and the necessity of moving from the category of sets to the category of generalized sets. The key idea is the partial element, induced by conflicting classifications. This idea is at the core of any subjective, multicriteria decision making.

THINKING IN RULES

Consider the following forward chaining.

(1) IF stain is gram-positive THEN organism is *Streptococcus*.

(2) IF strain is gram-negative THEN organism is *E. coli*.

(3) IF organism is *Streptococcus* or bacteroids THEN penicillin is indicated.

(4) IF penicillin is indicated AND patient allergies are unknown THEN ask about allergy to penicillin.

(5) IF penicillin is indicated AND NOT allergic to penicillin THEN prescribe penicillin.

Inference

When interpreted, this set of rules forms an inference network, which can be thought of as the executable image of a knowledge base, ready to be accessed by a driver. Such inference networks differ from simpler constructs, such as binary trees, in that each rule may be the parent of several rules and the child of several others. The lines connecting nodes in an inference network often cross. Such crossing is invalid in most simpler network constructs.

The major part of running a knowledge-based system is getting the driver program to load, interpret, and use the inference network. No predefined structure determines the relationship among rules; rules establish "hooks" to each other as they are loaded. This characteristic yields a fascinating property of inference networks: the rules that comprise them can be loaded in any order. That is, in the knowledge base of five rules, the inference network would be the same if the rules were loaded in the order 12345, 54321, or 24135.

A result of this property is that an inference network can be extended simply by adding new rules to the knowledge base, and these rules may be added at any location in the knowledge base. Thus, as more is learned about a particular field, the expertise of the knowledge-based system can be enhanced simply by adding new rules. Neither the driver program nor the original structure of the knowledge base need be altered provided that infinite chaining, introducing contradictions, and modifying existing rules are avoided.

Instantiation

Once a knowledge base is loaded and an inference network has been established, an initial state of the network is defined. The user can then introduce a fact in the system. For instance, in the case of the knowledge base of five rules, a fact could be

stain (gram-positive)
allergy (tetracycline)

As this new information is received, the driver analyzes it to determine which rules apply. The applicable rule is

IF stain is gram-positive THEN organism is *Streptococcus.*

Whenever the conditions for a rule match the state of the inference network, the action part of that rule is exercised. The action part of this rule is

organism is *Streptococcus.*

This sequence is known as instantiation. That is, a specific state of the network causes instantiation of another rule. In this case, the new rule is

IF organism is *Streptococcus* or bacteroid THEN penicillin is indicated.

The key to the system's intelligence is that each instantiation changes the state of the inference network and thus causes the future instantiation of other rules and the ultimate decisions the system makes. Any rule instantiation is a chain reaction, or ripple effect, in which the state of the inference network triggers instantiation of a certain rule, which in turn triggers the instantiation of another rule and so on.

After the driver program has assimilated the facts the user entered and has propagated the effects of these facts throughout the inference network, the system either makes a decision or asks the user for additional information. This cycle is repeated until a decision can be made.

In the example, the decision is

Prescribe penicillin

This decision is transparent; that is, the system can explain its decision. For instance, at the query

Why did you prescribe penicillin?

the system will answer

Because the stain is gram-positive (indicating *Streptococcus*), and the patient is not allergic to penicillin.

This answer is the result of the following steps:

stain (gram-positive)
IF stain is (gram-positive) THEN identify (*Streptococcus*)

id(strep)
IF id(strep) OR id(bacteroid) THEN indicated (penicillin)

ind(pen)
unknown allergic(pen)
IF ind(?drug) AND unk allergic(?drug) THEN ask allergic(?drug)

ind(pen)
NOT allergic(pen)
IF ind(?drug) AND NOT allergic(?drug) THEN prescribe(?drug)

A backward chaining is possible. At the query

What about prescribing penicillin?

the system will answer

Prescribe penicillin if the stain is gram-positive and the patient is not allergic to penicillin.

Degrees of Belief

Degrees of belief are the major currency of production systems. Production systems are based on repetitive use of the construct

IF *A* THEN *B*

This construct is applicable to situations in which there is usually only one correct decision. These are standard computer operations, and most computers have specific hardware components to speed them up.

Because we cannot be completely certain that some facts are true or that certain relations hold, each fact and each production rule are associated with a certainty factor (CF). The CF, a number in the interval $[-1,1]$, indicates the certainty with which each fact or rule is believed. Positive and negative CFs indicate a predominance of confirming or opposing evidence, respectively. CFs of 1 or -1 indicate absolute knowledge.

Inexact reasoning is based on the construct

IF *A* (to degree x) THEN *B* (to degree y)

Such constructs are applicable to decisions involving phenomenolog-ical data and situations in which there might be more than one correct decision. These are nonstandard computer operations and generally require extensive software support.

The difference between exact and inexact reasoning is best under-stood by example. Consider the following production rule:

IF (1) the infection is primary bacteremia
    (2) the site of the culture is sterile
    (3) the suspected portal entry of the organism is the gastrointes-tinal tract

THEN there is suggestive evidence (0.7) that the identity of the organ-ism is a bacteroid

Suppose the facts are represented as 4-tuples made up of an associative triple and its current CF, for instance:

$$(id, organism\#2, Klebsiella, 0.25)$$

To evaluate such production rules, one applies the following steps:

1. The CF of a conjunction of several facts is taken to be the min-imum of the CFs of the individual facts.

2. The CF for the conclusion produced by a rule is the CF of its premise multiplied by the CF of the rule.

3. The CF for a fact produced as the conclusion of one or more rules is the maximum of the CFs produced by the rules yielding that conclusion.

For example, consider these two rules, with respective CFs of 0.7 and 0.8, leading to conclusion D:

$$IF\ A\ AND\ B\ AND\ C\ THEN\ D\ (CF = 0.7)$$

$$IF\ H\ AND\ I\ AND\ J\ THEN\ D\ (CF = 0.8)$$

Additionally, suppose that the facts A, B, C, H, I, and J have CFs of 0.7, 0.3, 0.5, 0.8, 0.7, and 0.9, respectively. Then the following computation produces a CF of 0.56 for D:

$$min(CF_A, CF_B, CF_C) = 0.3\ (step\ 1)$$
$$0.3\ x\ 0.7 = 0.21\ (step\ 2)$$
$$min(CF_H, CF_I, CF_J) = 0.7\ (step\ 1)$$
$$0.7\ x\ 0.8 = 0.56\ (step\ 2)$$
$$max(0.21, 0.56) = 0.56\ (step\ 3)$$

The certainty factor formalism arose from the desire for a one-number calculus. Although CFs are not probabilities, they can be based on probability theory. Suppose you wish to use a production rule to decide whether you should take an umbrella when you leave home today. You might approach this decision with the following rule:

IF it is raining THEN take your umbrella.

A Bayesian approach (Heines, 1983) would be more complex, involving a number of factors that weight the decision one way or the other. Factors that indicate you should take your umbrella add positive values to a score of 0. Factors that indicate you should not take your umbrella add negative values to the score. In the final analysis, if the score is positive you will take your umbrella; if it is negative, you will not.

Factors that might add positive values to the score are:

80 It is raining when you leave home.
50 The weather report indicates rain.
30 Your spouse says it will rain.
20 You must wait outside for a bus.
20 The sky is overcast.
15 You are wearing new clothes.
15 You have meetings in other office buildings.
 5 You have just bought a new umbrella.

Factors that might add negative values to the score are:

−50 It is not raining when you leave home.
−40 The weather report indicates no rain.
−25 Your spouse says it will not rain.
−20 The sky is clear.
−15 You are wearing old clothes.
−15 You know that you will be staying inside today.
−15 You have lots of things to carry to work today.

Positive degrees indicate increasing probability that a hypothesis is true, while negative degrees indicate decreasing probability. These are subjective probabilities, and the relation between these subjective probabilities and the degrees of belief can be expressed as

$$\text{degree}(H) = 10 \times \log 10[\text{odds}(H)]$$

$$\text{odds}(H) = \frac{\text{prob}(H)}{1 - \text{prob}(H)}$$

as in the table

Degree of belief (CF)	Odds	Probability
− 30	1:1000	0.001
− 20	1:100	0.01
− 10	1:10	0.1
0	1:1	0.5
10	10:1	0.9
20	100:1	0.99
30	1000:1	0.999

PLAUSIBLE VERSUS APPROXIMATE REASONING: CHANGING THE TOPOS OF EVIDENCE COMBINATION

Evidence is indication; it is whatever makes clear the truth or falsehood of something. We described solutions for combining evidence derived from different premises or from different rules. These solutions are based either on heuristic or on formal methods, even if in most systems a trade-off between methods exists. Both heuristic and formal methods use numerical values for scoring conclusions and for indicating the strength of the rules.

A Bayesian link between premises and conclusions is defined by the weight with which the truth of premises supports the truth of conclusions. The difference between a logical link and a Bayesian link is that the former changes the degree of the conclusion to a specific value, while the latter changes the degree of the conclusion proportionately according to the weight of the link and the certainty of the user's facts.

In any probabilistic approach, these degrees are defined as measures of sets on a sample space. One assigns a number in the unit interval to a subset of existing events. We know from the beginning what the events are. They—the events—exist because they exist. The degree of belief is a measure of our knowledge about an occurrence whose existence is granted.

Certainty factors, or degrees of belief, are numbers that index a group of events forming a part of a universe discourse X. Any degree of belief is a value of the function

$$P(X) \rightarrow [0,1]$$

If we start with a known universe X, one number gives us an indication of the truth or falsehood of an inference. This is plausible reasoning.

Another approach to thinking about reasoning is to consider global evaluations of the entire universe of discourse. For instance, if we still want to use the unit interval as a reference order, such an evaluation could be a fuzzy set, the function

$$X \rightarrow [0,1]$$

In fact, this evaluation is equivalent to a family of crisp level sets chain-included. According to this representation, we assign to each index a level set defined as those elements of the universe for which the fuzzy set has a value greater than the index. In other words, the situation is

$$[0,1] \rightarrow P(X)$$

Such a family is a setlike object whose elements have degrees of existence. We now measure our knowledge about the existence of the elements of a set. Their degrees of existence are the degrees of our knowledge. If we start from an unknown reality or an imprecisely known reality, a function, and not a number, indicates the truth or falsehood of facts and inferences.

Plausible reasoning is based on one number that indicates degree of belief. Approximate reasoning is based on tables that include many numbers indicating degrees of existence. One number is enough to indicate a probability, but a function is needed to indicate a possibility.

The methodology of plausible reasoning is embedded in the world of sets. The methodology of approximate reasoning uses the framework of functions, or, more precisely, of setlike objects. When we leave the world of sets, which emphasize the element, to enter the world of setlike objects, which emphasize the function, we change the category.

THE THEORY OF CATEGORIES

The theory of categories is a good language for evidence combination. Any production rule, for instance

IF A THEN B

is a relation. No matter if we speak about exact reasoning, plausible reasoning, or approximate reasoning, this relation is an arrow

$$A \rightarrow B$$

A and B are different because the objects A, B have different natures; the key to understanding what they have in common lies in the way the arrow behaves. Consider this knowledge base as a collection of production rules.

$$\begin{array}{ll} \text{IF } A \text{ THEN } B & A \to B \\ \text{IF } B \text{ THEN } C & B \to C \\ \text{IF } C \text{ THEN } D & C \to D \\ \cdots\cdots\cdots\cdots & \cdots\cdots \end{array}$$

One can easily observe that

1. Each arrow is associated with two objects.
2. An operation of composition can be performed on certain pairs of arrows to obtain a new arrow.
3. Each object is associated with a special arrow, the identity arrow.

We can say, therefore, that a production system comprises

1. a collection of things called objects
2. a collection of things called arrows
3. an associative law assigning to each pair of arrows their composite. Given the configuration

$$\begin{array}{cccc} f & g & h \\ A \to B \to C \to D \end{array}$$

of objects and arrows, then

$$h \circ (g \circ f) = (h \circ g) \circ f$$

where $\circ$ means composition. In other words, a diagram of the following form always commutes.

4. an identity law, assigning to each object B an arrow $1_B : B \to B$ such that for any $f : A \to B$, $g : B \to C$ we have

$$1_B \circ f = f$$
$$g \circ 1_B = g$$

In other words, the following diagram commutes.

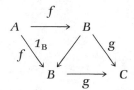

A knowledge base can be viewed as a universe of mathematical discourse determined by specifying a certain kind of object and a certain kind of arrow between objects. In approximate reasoning, the knowledge base can be viewed as the category whose objects are all functions

$$fz: A \rightarrow L$$

with the codomain L. An arrow from $fz: A \rightarrow L$ to $gz: B \rightarrow L$ is a function $k: A \rightarrow B$ that makes the triangle

commute; that is, $gz \circ k = fz$.

It is sometimes convenient to think of such objects as pairs (A, fz). Then the composition

$$(A, fz) \overset{k}{\rightarrow} (B, gz) \overset{m}{\rightarrow} (C, hz)$$

is defined as

$$m \circ k: (A, fz) \rightarrow (C, hz)$$

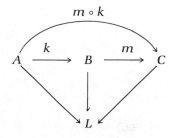

We are now ready to speak about evidence composition in a rigorous way. Consider the production rules

$$A \rightarrow C$$
$$B \rightarrow C$$

They form the diagram

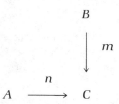

If we add a new object, P, and two arrows, m' and n', the pullback square

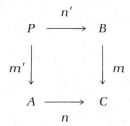

commutes, that is, $n \circ m' = m \circ n'$.

We say that n' arises by pulling back n along m, and m' arises by pulling back m along n.

A is one piece of evidence supporting a hypothesis C, and B supports the same hypothesis. P gives the evidence combination.

We can discuss more complicated diagrams. For instance, according to the pullback lemma from the theory of categories, if a diagram of the form

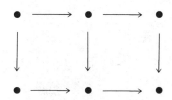

commutes, then:

1. If the two small squares are pullbacks, then the outer rectangle is a pullback.
2. If the outer rectangle and the right square are pullbacks, then the left square is also a pullback.

APPROXIMATE REASONING IN FUZZY OPTIMIZATION

Interest in the foundation of fuzzy system theory was heightened by difficulties with applying a conventional theory of multicriteria decisons. Efforts to understand and resolve these difficulties led to a study of classification and to new tools for modeling classification. The categorial language makes turning to representation from simple observation explicit—recognizing things by similarities instead of by differences.

Optimization Means Ordering

Since World War II, there has been an explosive development in quantitative methods of optimization but not too many attempts to discover fundamentals. The fuzzy set approach opened a door for such an enterprise.

In ordinary language, to optimize means to do the best one can under the circumstances. To refine this colloquial formulation into a mathematical statement, we must define *best* and *under the circumstances* precisely. If we take the word *best* to mean either *maximal* or *minimal*, then the problem is simplified significantly, and optimization becomes the finding of the maximal or the minimal value of some numerically valued function. In other words, an optimization problem consists of a set S and a function f such that S is in the domain of f and

$$f: S \to R$$

where R is the real line. The problem becomes finding some or all elements of S for which the function value is either maximum or minimum.

After giving this general definition, we must state immediately that the solutions of special instances of optimization problems constitute entire branches of mathematics in themselves. A good example is linear programming, the subject of many books. In linear programming, both the set S and the function f are severely restricted.

Thinkers in past years approached optimization systematically, using the the idea of natural order. By that means, they obtained rules for dealing with matters of great practical utility. If we examine the meaning of the function f, we see that the elements of the set S are mapped into numbers. In this way, the order structure of the real line can be used to define *best*. The order structure of the real line is therefore an instrument of our perceiving apparatus. When we observe its points, we perceive only two directions, ahead and behind; and these two directions are characterized by two relations, greater and lower. The points move in time along the real line, which is viewed as a space.

Two ideas underlie optimization: the idea of space and the idea of motion. An illustration from linear programming is a problem in which extreme points of a polyhedron representing some constraints are explored sequentially, and in which the exploration is guided by an objective function.

We must focus on the perceiving apparatus when we speak about the logic of optimization. Moving along the real line, we observe its elements. A two-valued logic is quite sufficient to assess the existence of any elements. The path that immediately opens before us is applying the same philosophy when another structure is used to define *best*. The following section shows, however, that when time is considered in its historical integrity, a multivalued logic is necessary to assess degrees of existence.

Any Logic Is Internalized in a Structure

Reformulating the standard optimization construction in the language of sets, one can say that the solution of any optimization problem is a subset of S as defined by the characteristic function

$$S \rightarrow \{0,1\}$$

The internal membership structure is characterized externally by reference to connections with a special set $\{0,1\}$ having only two elements. This correspondence between subset and characteristic function is shown by the following diagram

$$
\begin{array}{ccc}
solution & \longrightarrow & S \\
\downarrow & & \downarrow \\
\{0\} & \longrightarrow & \{0,1\}
\end{array}
$$

where the arrow $\{0\} \rightarrow \{0,1\}$ gives the meaning *true*. $\{0\}$ is a special set with only one element, to which only one arrow can be drawn.

Because the elements of the solution are uniquely linked with $\{0\}$, the diagram describes how elements in the solution are observed and selected from the elements of S according to a precise meaning of what is true. The set $\{0,1\}$ is a subset classifier, and its elements are the truth values of the logic of classification. If an element of S is in the solution, then the characteristic function takes the value 1; otherwise, it takes the value 0.

There are only two elements in the subset classifier: 0 and 1. One means *true*, and zero means *false*. *True* and *false* should not be taken in their literal or ordinary sense but more specifically to mean that a particular element of the real line R is set. Generally, we dispense with the clumsy "is true" or "is false" and say "equals 1" or "equals 0," respectively.

After this preamble, we can begin exploring multicriteria optimization. How do we solve a problem defined by many classifications, that is, by more than one ordering along the real line? The problem is not simple.

Consider a family of such classifications (solutions), no two of which have elements in common. That is, any two members of the family are disjoint sets. For each index $i \in I$, there is a set S_i that belongs to the collection. We can visualize these sets (solutions) as "sitting over" the index set I. A set over I is a fiber over i, and we have to consider a bundle of ordinary sets. The subbundle classifier is a bundle of set-classifiers $\{0,1\} \times I$, and the classifier arrow can be thought of as a bundle of copies of the set function *true*.

An element of the bundle is a global section $I \rightarrow S$ that picks one germ out of each fiber. Such elements are called *partial elements*. We might regard a bundle as a setlike entity consisting of potentially existing (partially defined) elements.

Let e_1 and e_2 be two partial elements of a bundle and let

$$/e_1 = e_2/ = \{i \in I, e_1(i) = e_2(i)\}$$

Then $/e_1 = e_2/$ as a subset of I is a truth value of the statement $e_1 = e_2$ or, alternatively, a measure of the extent to which an element e_1 "looks like" an element of e_2.

A generalized concept of *set* emerges—a set consists of (partial) elements, with some Heyting algebra-valued measure of the degree of equality of those elements.

Some Families of Crisp Sets
Can Be Modeled As Fuzzy Sets

Consider again the optimization problem

$$f:S \rightarrow R$$

Instead of observing and selecting the maximal (or minimal) values, consider representing all the elements of S ordered with reference to the extreme value of the function f. This can be achieved, for instance, by dividing all the values by the maximal (or minimal) value. This new ordering is governed by the unit interval

$$S \rightarrow R \rightarrow [0,1]$$

The new function fz

$$S \rightarrow [0,1]$$

is a fuzzy set, and according to the representation theorem is equivalent with a family of level sets $(S_i)_{i \in [0,1]}$

$$S_i = \{s:fz(s) \geq i, i \in [0,1], s \in S\}$$
$$S_i \subset S_j \Leftrightarrow j < i$$

Consider the fuzzy set given in this table.

A	0.9
B	0.8
C	0.7
D	0.6
E	0.5
F	0.4
G	0.3
H	0.2
I	0.1
J	0.0

The level sets of the table are:

A
$A\ B$
$A\ B\ C$
$A\ B\ C\ D$
$A\ B\ C\ D\ E$
$A\ B\ C\ D\ E\ F$
$A\ B\ C\ D\ E\ F\ G$
$A\ B\ C\ D\ E\ F\ G\ H$
$A\ B\ C\ D\ E\ F\ G\ H\ I$
$A\ B\ C\ D\ E\ F\ G\ H\ I\ J$

All the level sets are included in each other and form a "set-through-time."

$$\{A\} \subsetneq \{A,B\} \subsetneq \{A,B,C\} \subsetneq \ldots$$

The set-through-time is indexed by the membership degrees, which are the time of existence measured by the height of each column. The elements of the unit interval are, therefore, the truth values of an internalized logic in the category whose objects are sets-through-time.

Another way to look at level sets is to interpret the columns as sections of a bundlelike object indexed by the unit interval. Then, the heights of the columns can be measured by open sets in the unit interval, and the heights of the columns can represent the degree of equality between A, B, ... J, or the distance between them.

No matter how we consider the family of level sets, they are objects scattered in topoi. For this reason, we can use a non-two-valued logic to handle them by "fuzzy optimization."

Fuzzy Optimization Is Knowledge Engineering

The core of the theory of topoi models a classification that allows one to speak about partial elements. The theory can be difficult to use directly, however. Fortunately, there is an alternative—fuzzy sets modeling families of level sets. Using degrees of membership instead of degrees of existence allows a precise model for subjective evaluations. This is a turning point in the methodology of science.

Subjective means existing in the mind, belonging to the person thinking rather than to the object thought of. Any subjective evaluation is the result of a classification, conscious or not. Subjective evaluations and fuzzy sets are not one and the same, but instead relate as a goal does to a tool. Having precisely manipulable subjective evaluations is the goal, and fuzzy set theory is a tool to achieve the goal.

In any fuzzy programming model, knowledge is procedural in the sense that it tells how we can manipulate data to solve a problem. We can express knowledge in fuzzy programming as either constraints or objective functions. The basic building block of both constraints and objective functions is the predication, that is, an expression that says simple things about a universe of discourse. Predications are represented by fuzzy sets.

Once a set of constraints and objectives has been defined, we can use those constraints and objectives to deduce information. This is done by writing a query, an expression of the form

$$P_1 \text{ and } P_2 \text{ and } \ldots \text{ and } P_n$$

where P_i are predicates represented as fuzzy sets. Inference takes place automatically. The fact that answers are extracted from data descriptions by a logic procedure results in a great degree of data independence. Asking the knowledge base a question generates a knowledge tree. The answer procedure reduces the tree. The derivation of the knowledge tree from constraints and objectives is a forward process, while the evaluation process is a backward contraction process, a pullback in the structure of fuzzy sets.

In fuzzy optimization, "the best" is a new evaluation in the structure of all evaluations, pulling back toward a synthesis. Any fuzzy optimization problem is an exploration of a knowledge tree. The constraints are partial sources of knowledge or partial descriptions of a common universe of discourse—the universe of alternatives—and by conjunction complete knowledge is derived. This fact confirms the supposition that our idea of movement is essentially composite, containing two notions: the space of the evaluations and the time to explore this space.

The capacity to *represent evaluations* and the ability to *experience sets* leads to knowledge engineering. In classical optimization, logical operators are simply deduced from facts and embrace nothing but the content of facts. Operators are not laws of thinking but merely laws of the external world as we perceive it, or laws of our relationship to the external world.

SUMMARY

1. A category is a collection of objects and morphisms (arrows) between objects, satisfying an associative law.

2. The internalization of a knowledge base can be represented mathematically by a category whose objects are facts and whose arrows are rules.

3. A production rule

    IF A (degree x) and B(degree y) THEN C(degree z)

    can be represented by the diagram

4. To combine evidence degrees associated with facts, one can use a pullback square proper to the category of sets.

5. The symbolic manipulation of a production system exploits the associative law to chain the rules and the pullback diagram to combine the evidence.

6. Semantic manipulations are possible when the knowledge base internalizes additional arrows, representing the evaluation of meaning. Then, a production rule

IF A and B THEN C

can be represented by the diagram

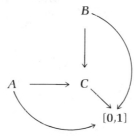

7. The operator AND is given by the mechanism of pullback square

proper to the category of fuzzy sets.

8. A fuzzy set is an evaluation that can be represented as a family of crisp sets. The category of families of crisp sets is included in the topos of generalized sets, whose logic is given by the truth values of a subobject classifier.

9. Approximate reasoning is based on the logic of fuzzy sets.

READINGS

Nau, D. S. 1983. Expert computer systems. *Computer* February: 63–85.

Nau discusses the techniques used in expert systems on the data level, on the knowledge-base level, and on the control level. The data level is declarative knowledge about the problem being solved and about current attempts to solve the problem. The knowledge-base level is knowledge specific to the problem that the system is set to solve. The system uses this knowledge, which often takes the form of operators or "pattern-invoked programs," to reason about the problem. One, many, or no operators may be applicable to the problem at any one time. If applied, an operator produces changes in the data. The control level includes a computer program that makes decisions about how to use specific problem-solving knowledge. Decisions are made, for example, about which operators to apply and how to apply them. Because expert systems use a combination of artificial intelligence, problem-solving, and knowledge representation techniques, information on these areas is included.

Computer. October 1983. Whole issue. Special issue on knowledge representation.

The contributors to this issue on knowledge representation are well-known researchers who met at a 1982 conference of the Canadian Artificial Intelligence Society. During the mid-1960s, knowledge representation slowly emerged as a separate area of study. Several different approaches began to take shape and led to the various formalisms of today. The most important current approaches are semantic networks, first-order logic, frames, and production rules. The attempt to make the semantics of knowledge representation precise is proceeding on several fronts. Work on nonmonotonic logic tries to extend predicate calculus to handle a wider variety of phenomena, and a distinguished effort is made to represent imprecise information.

Heines, J. M. 1983. Basic concepts in knowledge-based systems. *Machine-Mediated Learning* 1:65–95.

This article helps those not working directly in artificial intelligence to gain insight into the power and methods of that field and its potential use in learning systems. This paper discusses the Bayesian approach in a program called Advice Language/X (AL/X), a miniversion of MYCIN developed at the University of Edinburgh and supported by British Petroleum, Ltd.

Ishizuka, M., Fu, K., and Yao, J. T. P. 1982. Inference procedures under uncertainty for the problem-reduction method. *Information Sciences* 28:179–206.

These authors give a clear presentation of the inference procedure in expert systems. Unlike intuitive procedures employed so far in some expert systems, rational inference procedures, as described in this paper, are based on Bayesian theory and Dempster-Shafer's theory of evidence. These results are extended to include fuzzy knowledge. Fuzzy reasoning is given as an alternative to probabilistic approaches, which require idealized assumptions. The main criticism of expressing uncertain subjectivity probabilistically is that probabilistic approaches cannot deal with ignorance effectively.

Lesmo, L., Saitta, L., and Torasso, P. 1983. Evidence combination in expert systems. Report ISI-83/2, Università di Torino, Istituto Di Scienze Dell'Informazione, October 1983 (Extended version of a paper presented at the NAFIP-2 Workshop, June 1983, at Schenectady, New York.

These authors discuss some problems of representing uncertain knowledge and combining evidence degrees in rule-based expert systems. Some methods proposed in the literature are briefly analyzed with particular attention to subjective Bayesian probability (used in PROSPECTOR), confirmation theory (adopted in MYCIN), and Shafer's theory of evidence. The paper presents an integrated approach, based on possibility theory, for (1) evaluating the degree of match between the set of conditions occurring in the antecedent of a production rule and the input data, (2) combining the evidence degree of a fact with the strength of implication of a rule, and (3) combining evidence degrees arising from different pieces of knowledge. The semantics of the logical operators in possibility theory and in a new approach are considered and compared. Finally, such quantifiers as *at least N, no more than N,* and *exactly N* are defined.

Zadeh, L.A. 1983. The role of fuzzy logic in the management of uncertainty in expert systems. *Fuzzy Sets and Systems* 11:199–227.

Zadeh gives a constructive critique of existing expert systems, in which the fuzziness of the knowledge base is ignored because neither predicate logic nor probability-based methods provides a systematic basis for dealing with it. As a consequence, fuzzy facts and rules are generally manipulated as if they were nonfuzzy, leading to conclusions whose validity is questionable. In particular, Zadeh questions the universal assumption that if each premise is associated with a numerical certainty factor, then the certainty factor of the conclusion is a number that can be expressed as a function of the certainty factors of the premises. In general, this assumption is invalid, but becomes valid if the certainty factors are represented as fuzzy rather than crisp numbers.

Negoita, C. V. 1984. Structure and logic in optimization. *Control and Cybernetics.*

This paper is an attempt to explain where fuzziness is coming from. Optimization is viewed as a movement in an order structure. If optimization is described by a set and a function, there are two possible ways to consider it. If the set is seen as an object and the function as a transformation, then exploring sets means ranking elements in time, and a two-valued logic is sufficient for observation. Multicriteria optimization, however, requires a framework in which the pair set-function is an object. Substituting the world of sets with the world of their evaluations leads to partial membership and to a continuous logic by which to perceive that membership.

Schmucker, K. J. 1984. *Fuzzy sets, natural language computations , and risk analysis.* Rockville, Md.: Computer Science Press.

Determining the risk associated with a proposed endeavor appears to be extremely difficult. Schmucker believes these difficulties lie in overall complexity and inherent imprecision, both of which can be overcome to some degree if one has access to an intelligent risk-analysis utility that allows estimates of risk to be stated in natural language.

In six chapters—review of set theory, fuzzy set theory, natural language computation, psychological considerations of fuzziness, the fuzzy risk analyzer (FRA), and future research—the book describes such a tool and gives the reader the mathematical background necessary to understand a fuzzy, arithmetic-based algorithm used to manipulate natural-language expressions.

The FRA can compute the overall risk for a system composed of many components if the user can describe the system hierarchically. One merely climbs the tree of the decomposition, computing the risk of each interior node from the risk values of its descendants, until one arrives at the root node.

Schmucker's ideas about an intelligent risk-analysis utility were implemented by the Computer Security Research Group at George Washington University. An enhanced version is said to be used in some commercial risk-analysis evaluation carried out by Information Policy, Inc., a Washington-based consulting firm.

Basically, FRA has three major modules. The first translates natural language expressions to discrete fuzzy sets; the second combines these fuzzy sets according to the rules of fuzzy arithmetic to calculate a fuzzy set representing the risk of the entire system; and the third maps the resultant fuzzy set back to a natural-language expression.

The key idea is to build and exploit an internalized knowledge tree. Its derivation is a forward process, while evaluation is a backward contraction process, a pullback in the structure of descriptions. These descriptions are fuzzy sets—tables—and their transformations are governed by the logic internalized in the structure of all descriptions. Because any evaluation is an array of numbers, the 1820 epigraph Schmucker chooses—"Defendit numerus [literally, the number protects] is the maxim of the foolish; deperdit numerus [literally, the number ruins], of the wise"—seems strange. The author is not aware of the theorem of representation, which explains the difference between the logic of sets and the logic of families of sets (setlike objects). Otherwise, he would have noticed that there is safety in numbers, not ruin.

The book is a coherent and self-contained account of a body of techniques of considerable relevance to natural-language computations. Schmucker observes that the very core of fuzzy set theory, the degree of membership, is difficult to grasp and that, fortunately, the linguistic variable—a notion built on top of fuzzy set theory—is an alternative. He observes also that the terms *linguistic variable* and *fuzzy set* are not interchangeable; having precisely manipulable natural language expressions is the goal, and fuzzy set theory is a tool to achieve the goal. Finally, he observes that while fuzzy set theory (and in particular its use to represent linguistic variables) is relatively new, the goal of having something like a linguistic variable is rather old. As Schmucker observes, Leibnitz once said: "If we could find characters or signs appropriate for expressing all our thoughts as definitely and as exactly as arithmetic expresses numbers or geometric analysis expresses lines, we could in all subjects, insofar as they are amenable to reasoning, accomplish what is done in arithmetic and geometry."

Nalimov, V. V. 1981. *Faces of science*. Philadelphia: ISI Press.
Nalimov, V. V. 1982. *Realms of the unconscious: the enchanted frontier*. Philadelphia: ISI Press.

Nalimov, a well-known mathematician and cybernetician, is a member of the Scientific Council of Cybernetics and director of the Laboratory of Mathematical Theory and Experiment of Moscow State University. An expert in theoretical and applied statistics, he is in a favorable position to explore an important shift in modern science, the transition from the deterministic approach to the probabilistic one.

Robert Colodny of the University of Pittsburgh, the editor of these books, sees evidence of Nalimov's deep concern about the often strained relations between the sciences and the older humanistic traditions in Nalimov's attempt to show that culture of our epoch tends toward a single, unified vision of the world.

Randomness is regarded as a synonym for fuzziness as it is defined in the theory of fuzzy sets. It is noteworthy, says Nalimov, that the commonly accepted axiomatics of probability theory, proposed by Kolmogorov, lacks the notion of chance. Moreover, a broad use of probabilistic logic requires overcoming a very serious obstacle that is predetermined paradigmatically. Common, nonmetaphorical usage of the language of probabilistic concepts demands that both the space of elementary events and its metrics be given. Strictly speaking, however, one cannot say that the semantics of the psychology of thinking has any metrics.

By adopting a metaphorical language of probabilistic concepts, Nalimov lands in the field of fuzzy sets. The discrete and the continuous are not different sources of psychic existence, but only different manifestations of it. In other words, a person is one of the possible states of the semantic field. In perfect consensus with the recent researchers of the cybernetics of human systems (see Geyer and van der Zouwen, 1982), Nalimov sees individuality as determined by an evaluation—a distribution of truth values—and the dynamics of its progress as determined by its restructuring. If we adopt a categorial language, this restructuring is done by pullback in the structure of evaluations.

Starting from this point, Nalimov elegantly restores a principle seriously endangered by some of the confusions of the nineteenth century: "It is the scale that makes the phenomenon." An evaluation is a human phenomenon, and a human phenomenon will be recognized as such only if it is grasped at that level, if it is studied as something human.

This book is a remarkable work with deep implications for the philosophy of any fuzzy approach. For the first time in the philosophy of science, fuzzy set theory is viewed as a turning point.

CHAPTER THREE

Fuzzy Sets

The purpose of this chapter is to explain why fuzzy sets are important, to outline their theory, and to give some examples.

VAGUENESS

Without question, the explicit consideration of vagueness in natural language began with the ancient philosophers. They observed that an arresting but not disturbing feature of everyday language is the vagueness of its words. Instructive puzzles were constructed on this observation.

The following is a modernized version of a paradox called "sorites" (Black, 1970). We commonly distinguish men who are tall from those who are not. A man who measures 4 feet is short. A man does not stop being short because 1/10 inch is added to his height. Therefore, a man who measures 4 feet and 1/10 inch is still short.

If we continue arguing in the same pattern, adding yet another 1/10 inch to a short man's height does not change his status. Therefore, a man who measures 4 feet and 2/10 inch is still short. In this way, we can reach the absurd conclusion that a man whose height is 4 feet and 500/10 inches is short. For, if the first argument is sound, so is the second; and if the second is, so is the third, and so on. There appears to be no good reason for stopping at any one point rather than another. It is difficult to see why the chain of argument should ever be broken, but it is ridiculous to conclude, for example, that a man who measures 7 feet is short.

Almost no one considers a 6-foot man short. Almost everyone considers a 4-foot man short. In between, there is a gradual variation. The same argument applies to the number of grains in a heap of corn, the number of hairs on a man's head, and all cases in which it is hard to "draw a line."

Anybody confronted with the sorites argument can see that the puzzle arises from deficiencies in representing the concept *short* by a crisp set. Arbitrary divisions between tall and short, rich and poor, and so on will be unsatisfactory to anybody who is aware of gradual progression. The inductive step in the sorites paradox is unwarranted logically and mathematically if the concept *short* is represented by a crisp set. This speaks against using discrete categories to describe a continuum.

One might hope to escape the absurd consequences of the sorites argument by recognizing a division of men's heights into three, rather than two, classes. It is at least plausible to distinguish between men who are clearly short, men who are clearly not short, and the remaining men who are neither clearly short nor clearly not short. The last of these classes is commonly said to consist of borderline cases, which jointly occupy a fringe or penumbra. This way of looking at the relation of the concept to its instances is valuable in understanding the role of a new notion, that of a set without sharp borders.

Let us call a man who is within the penumbra, that is, a man who is neither clearly short nor clearly not short, a middle-sized man. The inductive premise, again, is, "A man does not stop being short because 1/10 inch is added to his height." Now that we have divided men into three classes, we must reject the inductive premise because adding 1/10 inch to some men's heights puts them over the line between short and middle-sized; that is, they will cease being clearly short and become borderline cases. In other words, we are forced to recognize a sharp boundary between the clear case and the penumbra. This is unacceptable.

It is a feature of our use of a vague concept, such as *short*, that there is no determinate point at which a transition from a clear case to a borderline case occurs. The occurrence of vague expressions thus testifies at once to the existence of experienced continua of qualities and dispositions and also to the absence of fixed habits of discrimination between segments of such continua.

We cannot draw a boundary, except arbitrarily, between cases when a word applies and cases when it does not simply because a continuum exists that makes it impossible to do so satisfactorily.

Sometimes, for one special purpose or another, we must draw a boundary even though we feel uncomfortable about it. Ordinarily we do not distinguish sharply between the meaning of the word *city* and that of the word *town*, but for statistical purposes the Bureau of the Census must draw a line somewhere, so it draws it at 2500. If a child is born in a town of 2499, the town becomes a city. In common usage, we do not draw such a sharp line because we see no justification for it. Increasing the number of lines from one to two—or, for that matter, to some larger number—does not help us avoid drawing any line. Thus, whenever we use vague concepts, we must be on the alert to represent and handle them properly. This applies to expert systems in which knowledge is represented and handled according to the rules of natural language.

Any attempt to rid our natural language of vagueness is chimerical. An essential characteristic of a vague predicate is that the boundaries of the domain of its applicability are not fixed, and, therefore, we do not know precisely where this domain ends and some other begins. The question of truth and falsity here is not only undecided but undecidable. A proposition whose nature implies the lack of a criterion for deciding its truth or falsity shows the inapplicability of the notions of truth and falsity used in the principle of the excluded middle. In other words, vague concepts cannot be handled according to classical, two-valued logic.

OPEN TEXTURE

Vagueness can be distinguished from open texture. A word used in a fluctuating way—such as *heap* or *pink*—is vague. A term such as *intelligent*, though not vague, is nonexhaustive or open-textured because we can never fill all the possible gaps through which a doubt may seep in. In other words, definitions of open terms are always corrigible or emendable.

Open texture is a fundamental characteristic of most empirical concepts, and this texture prevents us from verifying most empirical statements conclusively. The terms that occur in a statement are nonexhaustive. For this reason, we cannot foresee completely all possible conditions under which they could be used. There will always be a possibility, however faint, that we have not taken into account something that may be relevant to their usage, and thus we cannot foresee completely all possible circumstances under which the statement is true or under which it is false. There will always remain a margin of uncertainty. Thus, the absence of conclusive verification is directly due to the open texture of the terms used in statements.

Due to the open texture of the term *intelligent*, the statement "he is intelligent" cannot be reduced to a cojunction or disjunction of statements that specify the ways a man would behave in certain circumstances. A definition is no stronger than its weakest link. Every time we think we have an airtight rule, we discover that its constituents are not airtight. The plugs that fill the gaps are themselves full of holes.

This phenomenon is called the "open texture of language." This is just the way the language is. As long as words are defined with imprecise words, and those in turn with others, this phenomenon will continue. Even words devised for special purposes in the various sciences present difficulty.

To emphasize the diachronic aspect of open texture, we can use the idea of sets-through-time, that is, of the temporal dimension. An open term can capture a time contraction, and in this way we can speak about a distribution of possibilities. This generalization of ideas from constant to variable sets lies at the heart of open texture.

FUZZY SETS ARE FUNCTIONS

Classical set theory is governed by a logic that permits a proposition to possess one of only two values: true or false. This logic does not accord well with the need to represent vague concepts. We see things in shades of gray, not only in black and white.

The key idea in fuzzy set theory is that an element has a degree of membership in a fuzzy set. Thus a proposition need not be simply true or false, but may be partly true to any degree.

We usually assume that this degree is a real number in the interval [0,1]. Consider the fuzzy set "tall." The elements are men, and their degrees of membership depend on their heights. For example, a man who is 5 feet tall might have degree 0, a man who is 7 feet tall might have degree 1, and men of intermediate heights might have intermediate degrees. Different individuals will have differing opinions as to whether a given man should be described as tall. A possible representation could be

Height	Degree of membership
5'0"	0.0
5'4"	0.08
5'8"	0.32
6'0"	0.50
6'4"	0.82
6'8"	0.98
7'0"	1.00

According to this representation, the fuzzy set "tall" is defined by its domain—the range of values for heights (5′0″, 5′4″, 5′8″, ... , 7′0″) and the degrees of membership (0.00, 0.08, 0.32 ... 1).

A fuzzy set is an association between numbers, a correspondence that assigns to a given height one and only one number in the unit interval. It may be thought of as an evaluation, a subjective evaluation, applied to the heights to obtain degrees of membership. This is symbolized as

$$\text{tall: heights} \rightarrow [0,1]$$

"Heights" is the domain or source of "tall," and [0,1] is the codomain or target.

How does set theory deal with this notion? To begin with, we introduce the notion of an ordered pair, consisting of two objects, with one designated first and the other second. The essential property of an ordered pair (x, y) is that $(x, y) = (z, w)$ if and only if $x = z$ and $y = w$.

We now define a binary relation as a set whose elements are all ordered pairs. This definition formalizes the intuitive idea of an association referred to earlier. From a function we obtain the relation

$$\text{tall} = \{(\text{height, degree}):\text{degree is the tall-image of height}\}$$

To distinguish those relations that represent function, we have to incorporate the central feature of functions, namely that a given input produces one uniquely corresponding output. Thus, each height can be the first element of only one of the ordered pairs in "tall." That is

IF   (height, degree 1) $\in$ tall
AND   (height, degree 2) $\in$ tall
THEN   degree 1 = degree 2

This is the set-theoretical characterization of a function as a set of ordered pairs satisfying the above condition. What happens next is a ploy often used in mathematics; a formal representation becomes a definition. It is quite common, in many papers on fuzzy sets, to find near the beginning a statement to the effect that "a fuzzy set is a set of ordered pairs."

How successful is this set-theoretical formulation of the fuzzy set concept? Technically it works well and allows an easy development of the theory of approximate reasoning. But a number of rejoinders can be made. Some would say that the set "tall" is not a function at all but the graph of a function. In subjects such as topology and analysis, writers often explicitly distinguish the function from its graph.

One way to cope with this objection is to modify the definition of *fuzzy set* in the following way. First, we define the Cartesian product as the set of all ordered pairs whose first elements are in the domain and whose second elements are in the codomain. This permits the fuzzy set to be defined as a triple

(domain, codomain, relation)

where the relation from domain to codomain is the graph of the function such that the previous condition is satisfied. Thus, the domain and codomain are incorporated in the definition of a fuzzy set from the outset.

Although the modified definition does tidy things up a little, it still presents a function as basically a set of some kind—a fixed, static object. The modified definition fails to convey the operational aspect of the concept. One talks of *applying* a function to an argument and of a function *acting* on a domain. There is a definite impression of action, as evidenced by the arrow symbol and the source-target terminology, and by common synonyms for function, such as mapping. An essential part of the meaning of the word *function* is this dynamic quality, which the "ordered-pairs" definition does not convey. Perhaps the term *elastic constraint* was used frequently in the later literature for this reason.

Formally, we do not deal with fuzzy sets but with fuzzy subsets of a given set. A fuzzy subset of S is a function from S into [0,1]. Note that when the function can take on only the values 0 and 1, it can be regarded as the characteristic function of an ordinary, crisp subset of S. Thus, fuzzy subsets seem to be a generalization of ordinary subsets.

The generalization can go further if the unit interval is replaced by a lattice, by an object in a category, by the subobject classifier in a topos, and so on.

THE ALGEBRA OF FUZZY SUBSETS

We can now begin defining the nature of operations on fuzzy sets. Let us look first at *complementation*. In general, the complement of a set contains all things that are not in the set. If we think of a normal set as having a sharp, crisp boundary, then the set's complement is everything outside the boundary.

We usually define the complement of a fuzzy set as that set whose grade of membership is exactly 1 minus the grade of membership of the original set. Consider two representations of "tall" and "not tall."

Complementation

Tall		Not Tall	
5′0″	0.00	5′0″	1.00
5′4″	0.08	5′4″	0.92
5′8″	0.32	5′8″	0.68
6′0″	0.50	6′0″	0.50
6′4″	0.82	6′4″	0.18
6′8″	0.98	6′8″	0.02
7′0″	1.00	7′0″	0.00

It is difficult to justify this negation. One can observe, however, that "not tall" depends only on "tall," and in this way we recover the usual complementation when fuzzy sets are crisp sets, that is, when all membership degrees are equal to 1. Also, one can observe that membership in "not tall" becomes smaller as membership in "tall" increases, and that one recovers the original fuzzy subset by double negation. The above assumptions do not determine complementation uniquely, even if we observe that a certain change in the membership value of "tall" has the same effect on the membership of "not tall." Justification becomes even more difficult if we try to generalize the definition of a fuzzy set, for instance, by accepting a different structure as codomain. This is the case when one tries to find fuzzy sets in topoi.

At any rate, by complementation we have generated another fuzzy subset, "not tall," from the original fuzzy subset "tall." If we wish, we can assign a new label to the new fuzzy subset. We could choose the label "short," for example. This doesn't mean that "short" has to be a symmetric antonym of "tall." In general, it probably won't be. For our purposes, however, we will assume that "short" and "tall" are complementary fuzzy subsets as defined above.

Now that we have two fuzzy subsets, we can explore other operations on them. One is *intersection*. In classical set theory, the intersection of two sets contains those elements of the sets that are in one *and* in the other. But, by definition, an element of a fuzzy subset may be partly in one set and partly in another. Then, it cannot be more true that an element is in the intersection of two fuzzy subsets than it is true that it is in either one.

Thus, at any point in the domain, the truth of the proposition that an element is in the fuzzy subset "tall AND not tall" is the minimum of the truth of the propositions that it is in "tall" and that it is in "not tall." Because a fuzzy subset is a function, one can write

$$f_{\text{tall AND not tall}} = \min \left(f_{\text{tall}}, f_{\text{not tall}}\right)$$

The next table illustrates the intersection of the fuzzy subsets "tall" and "short."

Intersection	
Tall AND Short	
5′0″	0.00
5′4″	0.08
5′8″	0.32
6′0″	0.50
6′4″	0.18
6′8″	0.02
7′0″	0.00

Without considering the numbers, but just thinking about what we would mean by saying that a man is "tall and short," we can imagine that we would mean he is middle-sized. Thus, we would expect the highest membership degree to be in the middle of the domain, and the lowest to be at the edges, which is what we see in the table.

Of course, it is hard to imagine using the phrase "tall and short" to describe a person. Interestingly, though, descriptions generated by successive intersections of complemented fuzzy subsets, a more complex operation, do not always seem unnatural. The description "not tall and not short" seems more reasonable. From the fuzzy set theoretical point of view, the representations are equivalent.

More interestingly, one can derive new concepts by intersection. For instance, from "not tall" and "not short" we can obtain "middle-sized."

Not Tall			Not Short			Middle-Sized	
5′0″	1.00		5′0″	0.00		5′0″	0.00
5′4″	0.92		5′4″	0.08		5′4″	0.08
5′8″	0.68		5′8″	0.32		5′8″	0.32
6′0″	0.50	AND	6′0″	0.50	→	6′0″	0.50
6′4″	0.18		6′4″	0.82		6′4″	0.18
6′8″	0.02		6′8″	0.98		6′8″	0.02
7′0″	0.00		7′0″	0.00		7′0″	0.00

Now we can define the concept of *union*, the set of those elements that belong to either one or both of the constituent sets. For any point in the domain of two fuzzy sets, the membership of the union of the fuzzy subsets cannot be less than the membership of either component. Thus

$$f_{\text{tall OR short}} = \max\left(f_{\text{tall}}, f_{\text{short}}\right)$$

The next table illustrates union applied to the fuzzy subsets "tall" and "short."

Union	
Tall OR Short	
5'0"	1.00
5'4"	0.92
5'8"	0.68
6'0"	0.50
6'4"	0.82
6'8"	0.98
7'0"	1.00

We see that the membership function attains its highest values at the edges of the domain, and its smallest value at the center. Without considering the numbers, but just thinking about what we would mean by saying that a man is "tall or short," we can imagine that we would mean he is "not middle-sized."

Thus, we can derive new concepts by union also. For instance, from "tall" and "short" we can obtain "not middle-sized."

Tall			Short			Not Middle-Sized	
5'0"	0.00		5'0"	1.00		5'0"	1.00
5'4"	0.08		5'4"	0.92		5'4"	0.92
5'8"	0.32		5'8"	0.68		5'8"	0.68
6'0"	0.50	OR	6'0"	0.50	→	6'0"	0.50
6'4"	0.82		6'4"	0.18		6'4"	0.82
6'8"	0.98		6'8"	0.02		6'8"	0.98
7'0"	1.00		7'0"	0.00		7'0"	1.00

The following properties follow from the definitions of complementation, intersection, and union:

Commutativity

$$\text{tall OR short} = \text{short OR tall}$$
$$\text{tall AND short} = \text{short AND tall}$$

Associativity

$$\text{(tall OR short) OR middle-sized} = \text{tall OR (short OR middle-sized)}$$
$$\text{(tall AND short) AND middle-sized} = \text{tall AND (short AND middle-sized)}$$

Idempotency

$$\text{tall OR tall} = \text{tall}$$
$$\text{tall AND tall} = \text{tall}$$

Distributivity

$$\text{tall OR (short AND middle-sized)} = \text{(tall OR short) AND (tall OR middle-sized)}$$
$$\text{tall AND(short OR middle-sized)} = \text{(tall AND short) OR (tall AND middle-sized)}$$

Absorption

$$\text{tall OR (tall AND short)} = \text{tall}$$
$$\text{tall AND (tall OR short)} = \text{tall}$$

de Morgan's Laws

$$\text{not (tall AND short)} = \text{not tall OR not short}$$
$$\text{not (tall OR short)} = \text{not tall AND not short}$$

Identity

$$\text{tall OR undefined} = \text{tall}$$
$$\text{tall AND unknown} = \text{tall}$$

where "undefined" is the empty fuzzy set, a fuzzy subset having all membership degrees equal to 0, and "unknown" is the fuzzy subset having all membership degrees equal to 1, that is, the crisp set that serves as domain.

Involution

$$\text{not(not tall)} = \text{tall}$$

It is easy to see how new concepts can be derived according to these properties. Consider, for instance, the first example

tall AND short = middle-sized

According to de Morgan's laws

not (tall AND short) = not tall OR not short

and according to the rule of complementation

not tall OR not short = short OR tall

and according to the rule of commutativity

short OR tall = tall OR short

In this way, we find the second example once more

tall OR short = not middle-sized

The reader should note that so far we have spoken only about fuzzy subsets defined on the same domain, that is, on the same universe of discourse: "tall," "short," and "middle-sized" are all fuzzy subsets defined on the set of heights. Let us denote this set by H and all the fuzzy subsets that could be defined on H by $F(H)$

The set $F(H)$ together with the operations of intersection, union, and complementation form a Morgan algebra, an algebra where the law of excluded middle is no longer true. The reason is that "tall" and "not tall" overlap. The fact that complementation does not exist is an algebraic counterpart of the fact that the concept of belonging was modified. This circumstance can now be exploited to build new concepts by overlapping old ones. In a Boolean algebra representation, "tall AND not tall" cannot be defined. In a Morgan algebra, like that of fuzzy subsets, "tall AND not tall" means "middle-sized," and this makes all the difference in the world.

It is simple to justify the choice of "max" and "min" to define union and the intersection, respectively. The operators "max" and "min" are the only ones that exhibit the following necessary properties:

1. The membership degree in a compound fuzzy subset depends on the membership degree in the elementary fuzzy subsets that form it, but on nothing else.
2. The operators "max" and "min" are commutative, associative, and mutually distributive operators.

3. The operators "max" and "min" are continuous and nonde-creasing with respect to each of their arguments. The member-ship in "tall AND short" or "tall OR short" cannot decrease when the membership in "tall" or "short" increases.

4. Complete membership in "tall" and in "short" implies complete membership in "tall AND short." Complete lack of membership implies complete lack of membership in "tall OR short." In other words, $\min(1,1) = 1$ and $\max(0,0) = 0$.

At the beginning of the history of fuzzy sets, the assumptions above seemed to be consistent and sufficient to ensure the uniqueness of the choice of union and intersection operators. Later, a lot of research both from empirical and mathematical fields produced many other pro-posals.

One way to generalize the idea of operator is to investigate gen-eralized fuzzy sets, modifying the structure of their codomain. It is interesting to note that the two operators define a dynamics

$$\min: F(H) \times F(H) \to F(H)$$
$$\max: F(H) \times F(H) \to F(H)$$

in the structure of all fuzzy subsets $F(H)$ defined on the same carrier H. This movement is towards minimum and maximum elements. These elements exist because $F(H)$ is a lattice, and $F(H)$ is a lattice because the codomain of the fuzzy sets is a lattice (the unit interval).

HOW MANY ARE A FEW?
FUZZY NUMBERS AND SORITES REVISITED

Imprecise statements about quantities or magnitudes, for example, properties such as *many*, *large*, and *moderate*, are particularly inter-esting. All these properties can be regarded as fuzzy subsets of the real line whose elements are real numbers. Consider, for instance, the set of integers. Any addition operation can be considered as a function from the set of integers into the same set. Now, imagine that on the set of integers we have defined a fuzzy subset "many."

$$\text{many: integers} \to [0,1]$$

such that the membership function $f_{\text{many}}(n)$ is a monotonic function of n, with $f_{\text{many}}(0) = 0$ and $f_{\text{many}}(n) = 1$ for sufficiently large ns.

Such a fuzzy subset will induce another fuzzy subset by the addi-tion operation. To envision this fact, consider a possible definition of "many" given by the table

1	0.1
2	0.2
3	0.3
4	0.4
5	0.5
6	0.6
7	0.7
8	0.8
9	0.9
10	1.0
11	0.9
12	0.8
13	0.7
14	0.6

The membership degree for the number 18 can be obtained by observing that there are six possible ways to build this number:

$$9 + 9$$
$$10 + 8$$
$$11 + 7$$
$$12 + 6$$
$$13 + 5$$
$$14 + 4$$

All these numbers have degrees of membership in the fuzzy subset "many" defined above. When we add them, we have to take into account this fact, according to the rule of natural induction:

$$f_{many}(z) = \max_{x+y=z} \min(f_{many}(x), f_{many}(y))$$

Therefore, the membership degree of 18 is:

$$f_{many}(18) = \max(\min (f(9), f(9)), \min(f(10), f(8))$$
$$\min(f(11), f(7)), \min(f(12), f (6)),$$
$$\min(f(13), f(5)), \min(f(14), f(4)))$$
$$= \max(0.9, 0.8, 0.7, 0.6, 0.5, 0.4) = 0.9$$

Now imagine there are two fuzzy subsets on the real line, that is, two fuzzy real numbers completely defined by their membership functions, normal and convex. That means

$$\max f(x) = 1$$
$$x \geqslant y \geqslant z \text{ implies } f(y) \geqslant \min (f(x), f(z))$$

Their sum is another fuzzy number. For instance

$$\text{many: integers} \rightarrow [0,1]$$
$$\text{few : integers} \rightarrow [0,1]$$
$$(\text{many} + \text{few})(y) = \max_{y=u+v} \min(\text{many}(u),\text{few}(v))$$

The requirements of convexity ensure a piecewise continuity in the membership distribution. This requirement also implies that the points of the real line with the highest membership value will cluster around a given interval or point. This fact allows us to understand the semantics of a fuzzy number simply by looking at its distribution and also to associate it with a proper label, for instance "approximately 10." We are ready now to begin the paradox sorites. A small heap plus one stone is not a small heap, it is just a small heap plus one. First we make the observation that "small" has to be convex: one stone cannot be a heap, and two stones are only a couple. If we accept that a heap is five stones, then

$$
\begin{aligned}
(\text{small} + 1) &\neq \text{small} \\
(\text{small} + 100) &= \text{medium} \\
(\text{small} + 1000) &= \text{big} \\
(\text{small} + 10000) &= \text{huge} \\
(\text{medium} + 900) &= \text{big} \\
(\text{big} + 9000) &= \text{huge}
\end{aligned}
$$

because any crisp number can be regarded as having a degree of membership equal to 1. By addition, at one moment in time the carrier is shifted enough to cover a different interval of the real line.

THE CATEGORY OF FUZZY SETS

So far, we have handled only quantities and magnitudes. They were all defined on the same universe of discourse, the real line, a string of numbers. But fuzzy subsets can be defined on a variety of universes. For instance, the fuzzy subset modeling the concept *intelligent* can be defined on a set of individuals:

Intelligent

John	0.1
Peter	0.2
Harry	0.3
Mary	0.4

As usual, the fuzzy set structure is an assignment of a value in the unit interval to each point in an underlying set, in this case a set of names. We used the same technique to define magnitudes such as *tall*:

Tall

5'0"	0.00
5'5"	0.40
6'0"	0.50
6'5"	0.80
7'0"	1.00

which assigns numbers to numbers.

If we want to study correspondences between fuzzy subsets defined on different universes of discourse, we have to transform the underlying set mappings of these universes. For instance, between "intelligent" and "tall" we can observe a function of proportionality.

proportionality

intelligent ⟶ tall

We can define the function by a table.

John	7'0"
Peter	6'5"
Harry	6'0"
Mary	5'5"

This function preserves the order structure, because the induced point (7'0",1.00) in the graph of "tall" has a higher value than the corresponding pair (John,0.1) in the graph of "intelligent." This is valid for all the names in the universe of "intelligent." We say that there is a *morphism* between these two fuzzy subsets defined on different universes of discourse but with values in the same unit interval.

If we consider all the objects with the fuzzy set structure given by the unit interval and (more importantly) with a structure that preserves morphisms between those objects, we can speak about a *category of fuzzy sets*, conceived as a universe of mathematical discourse. And if understanding means reducing one type of reality to another, then by studying a category of fuzzy sets we can understand what semantic systems are, what they have in common, and what makes them useful in knowledge engineering.

The key lies in the way the morphisms behave. The operation of *composition* can be performed on certain pairs of morphisms to obtain a new morphism that is also in the category. This operation always obeys the associative law, which in turn allows the notion of *commutative diagram*, an important aid to understanding both category theory and knowledge engineering.

Knowledge diagrams are commutative diagrams according to a category of fuzzy sets. We say *a* category and not *the* category because the formal framework may be used for further explorations. At this level, the categorial approach plays a creative role. The systematization of the theory of fuzzy subsets with values in the unit interval may lead to new discoveries, or to a recognition of its similarities to other theories.

Consider the statement that a fuzzy subset is a generalization of a characteristic function that defines a crisp subset. In set theory, the power set $P(X)$, representing all the subsets of a set X, is often denoted 2^X. The latter symbol denotes the collection of all functions from X to $2 = \{0,1\}$. The justification for this usage is that a bijective correspondence exists between subsets of X and functions $X \rightarrow 2$. This isomorphism is established as follows: given a subset $A \subseteq X$, we define the function $f_A : X \rightarrow 2$, called the *characteristic* function of A, by the rule "For those elements of X in A, give output 1; and for those not in A, give output 0."

In the category of sets, the correspondence between subset and characteristic function is illustrated by a pullback diagram. The set A is the inverse image under f of the subset $\{1\}$ of $\{0,1\}$; that is, $A = f^{-1}(\{1\})$. Here is a pictorial representation:

This diagram represents a pullback square; that is, A arises by pulling back $\{1\} \hookrightarrow 2$ along f.

To generalize means to replace 2 by the unit interval. If we do so, we land in a well-known category called topos, which today is a classical framework for the categorial approach to logic.

The word *topos* ("place" in Greek) was used for any category whose structure is sufficiently like *Set*, the category whose objects are crisp sets and whose morphisms are the set functions. In topos, basic set-theoretical constructions behave much as they do in *Set* itself.

The notion of a topos has great unifying power. The idea that function rather than set membership is the fundamental mathematical concept has been entirely vindicated, but it also has ramifications for logic, the study of the canons of deductive reasoning. The principles of classical logic are represented in *Set* by operations on a certain set—the two-element, Boolean algebra. Each topos has an analogue of this algebra, and thus each topos has its own logical calculus. This calculus differs from classical logic. In general, the logical principles that hold in a topos are those of intuitionistic logic, which does not accept the principle of excluded middle.

If we replace 2 by the unit interval in the category *Set*, the new category, to be a topos, must have objects that are not *sets* but *sets-through-time*. We say that 2 was a subobject classifier for subsets in *Set*, and the unit interval is a subobject classifier in *Set*^{D}, the category of diagrams. In this category, the objects are chains of functions defined on sets whose elements change the membership in time.

In this way, an object in a topos is a setlike entity consisting of potentially existing (partially defined) elements, only some of which actually exist (are totally defined). This requires that elements exist before they be equal. A generalized concept of "set" begins to emerge: it is a collection of (partial) elements, with some Heyting algebra–valued measure of the degree of equality of these elements.

An *H*-valued set is defined, then, as an entity *A* comprising a set *A* and a function $A \times A \to H$, assigning to each ordered pair (x,y) of elements of *A* an element $/x = y/_A$ of *H*, and satisfying conditions for symmetry and transitivity.

A morphism from Λ to *B* in the category *H-Set* may be formulated as a function $f:A \to B$. Its graph would then be a subobject of $A \times B$ and so should correspond to a function of the form

$$A \times B \to II$$

We interpret the previous function as assigning to (x, y) the truth value

$$/f(x) = y/$$

giving the degree of equality of $f(x)$ and *y*; that is, a measure of the extent to which *y* is the *f*-image of *x*.

Intuitively, a subset of *A* may be represented by a function

$$s:A \to H$$

Such a function assigns to each $x \in A$ an element $s(x)$ of *H*, which we think of as the truth value of $x \in s$, or as a measure of the extent to which *x* belongs to the "set" *s*.

These ideas are not so strange as they seem at first. In fact, to make a "set" fuzzy, one has to make both the *membership* and the *equality* fuzzy. The moral to be drawn from these observations is that foundational studies are always necessary in a rigorous explication of the nature of mathematical reality. This involves a precise representation of mathematical concepts, so that their interrelationships can be clarified and their properties understood. Once systematized, the theory of fuzzy sets may be used in further explorations and compared to other theories.

The value of applying a rigorous scientific approach to these problems becomes clear. Objections to artificial intelligence, knowledge engineering, and approximate reasoning were often grounded in the belief that work in these fields is ad hoc, unscientific, and incapable of exhibiting sustained growth. The fuzzy set approach, open to categorial foundation, is a symptom of a changing situation.

SUMMARY

1. The key idea in fuzzy set theory is that an element has a degree of membership in a fuzzy set.

2. We usually assume that this degree is a real number in the unit interval, but other structures can be used as well to induce an evaluation structure on a universe of discourse.

3. A fuzzy subset of a universe of discourse U is a function

$$f{:}U \to [0,1]$$

4. On the set of all fuzzy subsets defined on the universe U, the following operations are defined:

$$(f \text{ OR } g)\ (x) \ = \ \max\ (f(x),g(x)) \qquad \text{union}$$
$$(f \text{ AND } g)\ (x) \ = \ \min\ (f(x),g(x)) \qquad \text{intersection}$$
$$f \subset g \text{ if and only if } f(x) \leqslant g(x)$$

5. These definitions are extensions of the definitions of ordinary sets.

6. Consider two universes of discourse U and T, and let F be a function from U into T. The image of a fuzzy subset f of U under F is defined by

$$(F(f))(y) = \max f(x)$$
$$F(x) = y$$

7. An extension of this definition to the functions of several variables is

$$(F(f,g))(y) = \max \min(f(x),g(z))$$
$$y = F(x,z)$$

8. A fuzzy number is a fuzzy subset of the real line such that

$$\max_x n(x) = 1$$

$$x \leqslant y \leqslant z \text{ implies } n(y) \geqslant \min(n(x),n(z))$$

9. Algebraic operations on fuzzy numbers can be defined using the definition of a function of several variables:

$$(f + g)(y) = \max \min (f(u), f(v))$$
$$y = u + v$$

In this way, a fuzzy arithmetic can be developed, although not all the operations are well-behaved, and their manipulation requires some care.

10. The aim of foundational studies is to produce a rigorous explication of the nature of fuzzy subsets.

11. The study of fuzzy subsets within category theory means that the concept morphism, abstracted from the concept function, may be used instead of the set membership relation. Instead of defining properties of collections by reference to its members, one can refer to its external relationships with other collections.

READINGS

Zadeh, L. A. 1965. Fuzzy sets. *Information and Control* 8:338–353.

This paper introduces the idea of modeling predicates via fuzzy subsets with values in the unit interval.

Goguen, J. A. 1968. Categories of fuzzy sets: applications of non-Cantorian set theory. Ph.D. thesis, Dept. of Mathematics, University of California, Berkeley.

This thesis of great influence explores the possibility of replacing the unit interval by some more general structure, such as a completely distributive lattice.

Kaufmann, A. 1975. *Theory of fuzzy subsets*. New York: Academic Press.

Kaufmann's extensive presentation of the basic concepts prepares those with little or no previous knowledge of this field for work with advanced and specialized texts. Although written as applied mathematics, it does not demand an advanced mathematical background and contains many examples and exercises. It represents the first volume of five published in French by Masson (Paris).

Negoita, C. V., and Ralescu, D. A. 1975. *Applications of fuzzy sets to system analysis.* Basel, Switzerland: Birkhauser Verlag, and New York: Halsted Press.

This compact presentation of the algebraic theory of fuzzy subsets introduces the so-called theory of representation. Any fuzzy subset is viewed as a family of crisp level sets, and in this way the relation between fuzzy structures and classical structures is studied. The book is not elementary, but for readers in fields where awareness of fuzzy mathematics is essential. Presentation of mathematics is rigorous; propositions are stated and proved.

Dubois, D., and Prade, H. 1980. *Fuzzy sets and systems.* New York: Academic Press.

This detailed, exegetical study of many relevant texts emphasizes the theory of fuzzy numbers. The book has five parts: introduction, mathematical tools, fuzzy models and formal structures, systems-oriented fuzzy topics, and a survey of potential applications. The book does not seek to embed fuzzy set theory in a pure mathematical framework.

Gupta, M., Saridis, G., and Gaines, B., eds. 1977. *Fuzzy automata and decision processes.* Amsterdam: North-Holland.

Of special note is a bibliography of 1150 items with each key word indexed and about 750 classified as related to fuzzy systems theory and its applications. The remaining items deal with closely related topics in many-valued logic, linguistics, and philosophy of vagueness. These background references are annotated in an initial section that outlines the relationship of fuzzy set theory to other developments and suggests various possibly fruitful interrelationships.

Negoita, C. V., 1981. *Fuzzy systems.* Tunbridge Wells, England: Abacus Press.

This book is intended neither as a treatise on the field, a critique of the work of other schools, nor a comparative evaluation of the success and failure of different approaches to the subject. It is intended to set forth in an orderly manner the motivations and viewpoints of a school of thought that cherishes the belief that the field of fuzzy systems can and should be discussed with mathematical skill. A chapter is devoted to the categorial approach with a section dealing with fuzzy sets in topoi.

Goldblatt, R. 1979. *Topoi: the categorial analysis of logic.* Studies in Logic and the Foundations of Mathematics, vol. 98, ed. Barwise et al. Amsterdam: North-Holland.

The purpose of this book is to introduce the reader to the notion of a topos and to explain its implications for logic and mathematics. It is a beautifully written, judiciously chosen course with elementary expositions. The facts and ideas are clear and readily comprehensible. A chapter is devoted to H-Sets.

Bernard, N. 1981. A contribution to a theory of fuzzy sets: multisets. Ph.D. Thesis, Dept. of Mathematics, University Claude-Bernard of Lyons, France (in French).

This excellent discussion of both features and defects of existing foundational studies in fuzzy set theory is oriented along the idea of "sets-through-time" with the intention to avoid the constraints imposed by a fixed universe of discourse and a fixed evaluation structure.

Discussions about embedding fuzzy sets in a topos seem to have started in 1978. Eytan exploited the idea soon thereafter. Pitts, Ponasse, and Carrega analyzed his attempt. The following papers are particularly important to the development:

Negoita, C. V., and Stefanescu, A. 1978. Fuzzy objects in topoi: a generalization of fuzzy sets. *Bull. Polytechnic Ins. Jassy* vol. 28.

Negoita, C. V. 1982. Fuzzy sets in topol. *Fuzzy Sets and Systems* 8:93–99.

Negoita, C. V., and Roman, R. 1980. On the logic of discrete systems dynamics. *Kybernetes* 9:189–92.

Pitts, A. M. 1982. Fuzzy sets do not form a topos. *Fuzzy Sets and Systems* 8:101–104.

Stefanescu, A. 1981. The category Set$_f$ as a topos. *Busefal* Printemps.

Eytan, M. 1981. Fuzzy sets: a topos logical point of view. *Fuzzy Sets and Systems* 5:47–67.

Cerutti, U. 1982. A categorial point of view in fuzzy theories. *Report.* University of Torino, Italy.

Ponasse, D. 1981. Remarques sur la catégorie Fuz(*H*) de M. Eytan. *Busefal* Printemps. (Published in English in *Fuzzy Sets and Systems 1983.)*

Carrega, J. 1981. Les catégories Set*H* et Fuz*H*. *Busefal* Printemps. (Published in English in *Fuzzy Sets and Systems* 1983.)

CHAPTER FOUR

Knowledge Representation

A representation is defined as a set of conventions for describing things. Most people working in artificial intelligence agree that designing a good representation is the key to solving difficult problems.

The knowledge of an area of expertise is generally of three types: facts, rules of good judgment (heuristics), and evaluations. Much problem-solving knowledge can be represented in the form of quanta called structures. Usually, these structures are propositions, production rules, and frames.

A proposition is a statement that asserts the value of a variable; for instance, "Harry is tall." A production rule is a statement with two parts: a situation recognition part and an action part; for instance, "John is tall implies John is heavy." This is an IF-THEN structure; the IF part is a list of things to watch for, and the THEN part is a list of things to do. A frame is a structure that ties together knowledge about a variable. It is composed of a set of descriptors and values that specify the variable; for instance, "John, weight, height." Thus defined, a collection of frames is simply a relational data base.

Any proposition, production, rule, or frame can be used individually or in systems of propositions, production rules, or frames. Recently, combinations of propositions, production rules, and frames, coupled with their evaluations, have been tried as a response to the increasingly felt need for more representational power. This is particularly true in logic programming.

Propositions, production rules, and frames allow unplanned interactions with facts. Such interactions are not possible with control structures based on predetermined interactions. A fact can be applied whenever appropriate, not just whenever a programmer predicts it could be appropriate.

Any proposition, production rule, or frame can be used individually or coupled with a subjective evaluation. A central axiom of knowledge engineering is that the knowledge system should have direct, manipulatory access to the knowledge, as opposed to having the knowledge built-in.

The explicit representation of evaluations in a knowledge base permits the building of systems that can assimilate and exploit quantities of knowledge larger than those practically incorporated in standard computer programs. Logic programming allows the manipulation of evaluated facts even in the absence of rules.

Usually, knowledge is derived in linguistic form from experts. The theory of fuzzy sets offers a way to incorporate subjective evaluations in knowledge bases. A linguistic variable differs from a numeric variable in that its values are not numbers but words. Fuzzy set theory is a tool to achieve the goal of having precisely manipulable natural language expressions.

THE PROBLEMS OF KNOWLEDGE ENGINEERING

Knowledge engineering—the activity of constructing a knowledge base and the inference procedures required to interpret it—is defined either as the subfield of artificial intelligence concerned with the acquisition, representation and application of knowledge or as the engineering discipline whereby knowledge is integrated into computer systems to solve complex problems normally requiring a high level of human expertise.

Anyone desiring to create a knowledge base, regardless of the specific domain involved, must deal with the following fundamental problems:

1. The problems of *knowledge representation:* How do we represent human knowledge in terms of data structures that a machine can process?

2. The problem of *inference generation:* How do we use these abstract data structures to generate useful information in the context of a specific case?

3. The problem of *knowledge acquisition:* How do we translate human knowledge as it currently exists in texts and the minds of domain experts into usable abstract representations?

To solve these problems simultaneously, we must satisfy two requirements:

1. *The modular requirement:* During the development of the knowledge base, experts are unlikely to present all the facts and relationships necessary for expert performance in the domain.

Being human, experts tend to forget or to simplify details about their knowledge, and the systems must augment their knowledge at a later time. Because knowledge imparted to the system is largely empirical and because knowledge in the domains is developing rapidly, systems need to make changes easily and in an incremental or modular fashion.

2. *The programming requirement:* The fundamental use of a programming system is not to create sequences of instructions for accomplishing tasks but to express and manipulate descriptions of computational processes and the objects on which they are carried out. A new generation of programming tools is being used in knowledge systems. These tools reflect the attitude that what we say in a program should be primarily declarative, not imperative.

The above requirements are compatible with and lead to the *natural language paradigm.* Domain experts should be able to use a knowledge base directly during knowledge acquisition as well as during exploitation. Thus, the knowledge system will support high-level representation languages whose primitive elements are the attributes and associations of a particular domain problem rather than programming concepts. Nonprocedural languages, embedding natural language, are intended to be comprehensible to a domain expert with little or no previous experience.

This approach contrasts with the traditional symbolic approach, in which a knowledge engineer serves as an intermediary between the knowledge base and its author. The idea of direct usability by domain experts using natural language is a key theme of this book. This idea motivates the research in fuzzy systems theory.

Most researchers have approached incremental construction and declarative programming by means of production rules knowledge representation. Each production rule has the form

$$\text{antecedents} \rightarrow \text{consequents}$$

If the antecedents are true, then the consequents are true with some certainty. The inference mechanism in a production system is a rule interpreter that applies the rules in the knowledge base to particular cases. The approach to generating new information is deductive. At any point in the deductive process, the rule interpreter must select which rule to evaluate. The interpreter can be antecedent-driven or consequent-driven. If it is antecedent-driven, the occurrence of one or more antecedents triggers the application of a rule to infer its consequents. If consequent-driven, the interpreter, in attempting to establish a certain fact, selects a rule with that fact as a consequent and then tries to verify it by confirming that the antecedents are present. There are several methods for propagating the measures of uncertainty from one rule to the next during rule evaluation. The fuzzy set approach is based on the representation of the meaning of the linguistic propositions.

Another approach to developing knowledge bases involves associative knowledge. Associative knowledge is typically represented in data structures called frames, which have been suggested as a model of human memory organization. Frames allow knowledge to be represented in a tablelike way that is familiar to everybody. Unfortunately, this improvement in representation techniques is partially compromised by the limitations of existing methods for processing knowledge organized in tables. The fuzzy set approach seems to solve this problem.

The power of expert systems lies in their knowledge bases. Moving knowledge from the brains of experts into computer programs is now largely a slow process of knowledge engineers working together with experts. Therefore, we seek more automatic methods for transferring and transforming knowledge into its computer representation. Exploiting verbal models for the automatic representation of knowledge holds much promise. By simulating the behavior of verbal models when we handle linguistic values, we can add new production rules to the knowledge base. Optimization generates an interesting class of verbal models. Fuzzy linear programming is now sufficiently developed to allow the use of verbal models for automatic transfer of knowledge. This is the topic of Chapter Six.

PRODUCTION SYSTEMS FOR SYMBOLIC MANIPULATIONS

Now we turn to a system of production rules to learn some points of reasoning style and practice. Consider a knowledge base of production rules to perform test interpretations. Such a knowledge base consists of a set of variables, such as CAPACITY, WEIGHT, EFFORT, and a set of rules, such as

> IF   (1) CAPACITY of JOHN is BETWEEN GOOD and VERY
> GOOD
> (2) WEIGHT is GREATER THAN MEDIUM
> THEN   there is suggestive evidence that EFFORT is moderate
>
> IF   EFFORT is KNOWN
> THEN   PERFORMANCE can be APPROXIMATED

In symbol manipulation systems, the premises are combinations of one or more clauses, each constructed of a predicate function with an associative triple (attribute, object, value) as its argument. For example, the first clause in the first rule above is

MEMBF	JOHN	CAPACITY	GOOD
predicate	object	attribute	value

MEMBF is a predicate, and the associative triple says that the CAPAC-ITY of JOHN (a person, in this case) is a member of the class GOOD. A standardized set of domain-independent predicate functions and a range of domain-specific attributes, objects, and associated values form the vocabulary of primitives for constructing rules. Usually, the rules are written in LISP, and each rule is an executable body of LISP code. The English version is generated automatically from templates, stored with each predicate function, that indicate the roles of the attribute-object-value triple. For instance, the template for the predicate BETWEEN used in the first sample rule is described as follows:

> Function template (BETWEEN   NUM1   NUM2   NUM3)
> Translation "NUM1 is between NUM2 and NUM3."

A rule premise is always a conjunction of clauses, and the action part indicates one or more conclusions that can be drawn if the premises are satisfied, making the rules purely inferential.

The rules are usually judgmental; that is, they make inexact inferences on a confidence scale. The conclusions, therefore, are evaluated by certainty factors. Standard statistical measures were rejected in favor of certainty factors because experience with human experts shows that experts do not use information in a way compatible with standard statistical methods.

Certainty factors are a measure of the association between the premise and action clauses in each rule and indicate how strongly each clause is believed. When a production rule succeeds because its premise clauses are true, the certainty factors of the component clauses are combined. The resulting certainty factor is used to modify the certainty factor specified in the action clauses. Thus, if the premise is believed only weakly, conclusions derived from the rule reflect this weak belief. Also, because the conclusion of one rule may be the premise of another, reasoning from premises with less than complete certainty factors is commonplace. Some models of inexact reasoning in symbolic manipulation systems permit one attribute to have several plausible values if the evidence so suggests.

To summarize, there are two major forms of knowledge representation in symbolic manipulation systems based on production rules: (1) the attributes, objects, and values that form a vocabulary of domain-specific conceptual primitives, and (2) the inference rules expressed in terms of these primitives and certainty factors, which are numbers. No attempt is made to model the meaning of the primitives.

PRODUCTION RULES CAN BE DERIVED FROM VERBAL MODELS

Today, knowledge engineering is governed by two major principles. The first is that the problem-solving power of a symbolic knowledge system is primarily a consequence of its knowledge base and only secondarily a consequence of the inference method employed. In other words, expert systems must be knowledge-rich even if they are meth-ods-poor.

The second principle is that this knowledge, as experience has shown, is largely heuristic, that is, judgmental, experiential, and uncertain. This knowledge can be extracted in chunks from an expert. Each chunk becomes a production rule that represents the expert's answer to a what-if question. The question may be posed by the expert, by the system designer, or *by the system itself.*

The third possibility is examined in this section, which explores the concept of quantitative analysis with linguistic values. The idea is to simulate a verbal model; that is, a list of verbal assignment statements ordered so that all independent linguistic variables in a given statement have been assigned linguistic values in preceding statements.

A simulation of a verbal model supplies initial linguistic values for the input linguistic variables and then uses the model statements to compute the linguistic values of the output linguistic variables.

To get a feeling for verbal models, consider a perfectly nonpresumptuous dynamic model for simulating a learning process (Wenstop, 1975):

LEARNING   ←   READING MINUS FORGETING

KNOWLEDGE   ←   KNOWLEDGE PLUS LEARING

FORGETTING   ←   ((INCREASINGLY GROWING) WITH LEARN-
                           ING) PLUS FALLING WITH KNOWLEDGE

The parentheses enclosing blocks of meaning remove ambiguity.

It is not easy to measure the variables numerically. READING, for instance, is a variable with a clear—although not precise—meaning. It can be intuited to have low or high values; but if the values are to be numeric, the variable must be defined operationally. This is difficult to do while preserving the intuitive content.

People willingly and readily judge READING as "high," "very high," or any other suitable linguistic value. There is no way to pinpoint the meaning of values by a number, but modeled as fuzzy sets such values can be represented by strings of numbers; that is, by arrays.

A necessary component of any semantic system is a means to represent meaning by machine. To find the meaning of composite expressions, we need a system for representing the meaning of the parts of an expression and rules for combining these parts into the meaning of the total expression. To achieve such a system, we have to build a vocabulary, a syntax, and a semantics.

If we represent the meaning of a linguistic value as a number array, we can think of the positions in the array as positions on a scale where the leftmost position corresponds to the lowest value and vice versa. The numbers are the possibilities that a position is included.

Models of the meaning of the four primary terms are shown below.

HIGH	0	0	0	0	0	0	0.1	0.3	0.7	1	1
LOW	1	1	0.7	0.3	0.1	0	0	0	0	0	0
UNDEFINED	0	0	0	0	0	0	0	0	0	0	0
UNKNOWN	1	1	1	1	1	1	1	1	1	1	1

The positions of the elements in the arrays represent corresponding points in the universe of discourse. The numbers represent degrees of membership of these points. In this way, we model the meaning of linguistic values as fuzzy subsets of an appropriate psychological continuum.

We assume that the semantic contents of each word in the vocabulary is independent of context. This assumption is not necessary, but it simplifies things considerably. It also may not be wholly unreasonable in view of the fact that we operate exclusively within the realms of psychological continua. It is thus natural to interpret primary terms through *constant fuzzy subsets.*

Hedges such as *very* and *rather* are assumed to operate only on membership values; that is, their effect is independent of the positions of the operand in the universe of discourse. Examples of their effects are shown below.

HIGH	0	0	0	0	0	0	0.1	0.3	0.7	1	1
VERY HIGH	0	0	0	0	0	0	0	0.1	0.5	0.9	1
RATHER HIGH	0	0	0	0	0	0	0	0	1	0.2	0

The hedges are therefore syntactically equivalent and may be referred to as *monadic semantic operators* because they modify what follows in the expression. All other words are seen to operate on the combined meaning of what is on either side. These words, such as *minus, plus,* or *with* may be referred to as *dyadic semantic operators.*

We are now in the fortunate position of being able to equate the three syntactic categories of vocabulary to the APL categories of constants, monadic functions, and dyadic functions. A semantic model may therefore be defined by specifying words as appropriate APL constants, monadic functions, or dyadic functions. If this is done, any verbal assignment statement will also be an APL statement.

APL is a language for describing procedures in information processing. It is used for programming in its ordinary sense—directing a computer to process alphanumeric data. Defining the words of the vocabulary as APL functions enables the computer to execute commands in natural language. In this way, we can tell the computer what to do in natural language. In turn, the computer can tell us what it has done, also in natural language.

With a vocabulary in the form of an APL program package, we can perform quantitative analysis with linguistic variables. In other words, we are able to simulate—to answer what-if questions. Answering a what-if question means building an IF,THEN statement; that is, a production rule.

Let us, for the purpose of illustration, simulate the linguistic learning model for some selected initial values. Assume that we initially have

$$\text{KNOWLEDGE} \leftarrow \text{LOW}$$

$$\text{FORGETTING} \leftarrow \text{LOW}$$

If READING has a constant HIGH value, KNOWLEDGE will be MEDIUM. We can state, therefore, that

IF (1) READING is HIGH
   (2) at the beginning KNOWLEDGE is LOW
   (3) at the beginning FORGETTING is LOW

THEN there is suggestive evidence that later KNOWLEDGE will be MEDIUM.

This piece of knowledge will be evoked from the knowledge base if the conditions are true and will be built into the line of reasoning if necessary.

The system uses linguistic values as input, and the output is also linguistic values. The input-output characteristics of the system are acceptable by reasonable natural language standards. In other words, fuzzy set technology yields realistic norms for manipulating linguistic values. The norms are realistic to the extent that people would agree that natural language could be used more or less this way if it were employed systematically in quantitative analysis. With the exception of propositional calculus, natural language had not been used this way until the advent of fuzzy set theory.

The reader should understand how vector representation can be changed back into linguistic representation. The term *linguistic approximation* arises in that context and requires explanation. That understanding hinges on some understanding of elementary programming, however, and for now we necessarily work from the notion of linguistic variable upward toward abstractions, not downward toward implementation techniques.

PRODUCTION RULES ARE RELATIONS BETWEEN FUZZY SETS

Consider again the fuzzy subsets "tall" and "not short" as defined in Chapter Three.

Tall		Not Short	
5'0"	0.00	5'0"	0.00
5'4"	0.08	5'1"	0.08
5'8"	0.32	5'8"	0.32
6'0"	0.50	6'0"	0.50
6'4"	0.82	6'4"	0.82
6'8"	0.98	6'8"	0.98
7'0"	1.00	7'0"	1.00

We can say

IF tall THEN not short

This is an *implication,* a statement about a link. We say that these two fuzzy subsets are in relation. If we question their degree of relation, we have to remember that every element in these fuzzy subsets has its own degree of membership. The element 5'0" in "tall" has a degree of membership of 0.00, and the same element in "not short" has the same degree of membership. Judging pointwise, we say that the relation between these two points is 0.00.

Now, consider the implication

IF tall THEN not middle-sized

The element 5'0" in the fuzzy subset "not middle-sized" has a degree of membership 1.00.

Not Middle-Sized	
5'0"	1.00
5'4"	0.92
5'8"	0.68
6'0"	0.50
6'4"	0.82
6'8"	0.98
7'0"	1.00

Clearly, their relationship has a degree of 0.00. The element 7'0" has a degree of 1.00 in both fuzzy subsets. We say that their relation has a degree of 1.00. The element 5'8" has a degree of 0.32 in "tall" and of 0.68 in "middle-sized." We say that they have a degree of relation of 0.32; that is, not more than the minimum. This is so because, according to the properties of fuzzy set algebra, this implication can be written

IF tall THEN (tall OR short)

and be analyzed further according to the rule of absorption, according to which

tall AND (tall OR short) = tall

So far we have discussed only fuzzy subsets defined on the same universe of discourse. What happens when these universes are different? We shall keep the fuzzy subset "tall" and consider a second one, "heavy," defined on the set of weights. For instance:

Heavy	
100	0.00
140	0.00
180	0.18
200	0.50
240	0.98
280	1.00
300	1.00

From the beginning, the reader should notice that "heavy" has the same general shape of membership function as "tall." We might feel that there is an approximate relationship between height and weight. If we know only that a person is tall and have to guess at that person's weight, then the safest general assumption is "the taller, the heavier," recognizing that there are many counter examples.

For the moment consider the implication

IF tall THEN heavy

To use this statement in practice, we need to define an operation so that for any element in the domain "tall" we can generate the equivalent element in the domain "heavy." Then, given a height, we can deduce the most possible value for weight.

We first consider "tall," the premise, and establish the degree of membership of the premise value within the fuzzy subset. For example, looking at the definition of "tall" we see that a height of 6'0" has a degree of membership of 0.50. We can take the view that the degree of membership of the conclusion "heavy" cannot exceed the degree of membership of the premise.

Using this rule, we can set up a square array (the relation) composed of the premise and the conclusion membership functions in such a way that each element is the minimum of the values of the membership functions forming the axes of the array.

Tall	Heavy (100) 0.00	(140) 0.00	(160) 0.18	(200) 0.50	(240) 0.98	(280) 1.00	(300) 1.00
(5'0") 0.00	.00	.00	.00	.00	.00	.00	.00
(5'4") 0.08	.00	.00	.08	.08	.08	.08	.08
(5'8") 0.32	.00	.00	.18	.32	.32	.32	.32
(6'0") 0.50	.00	.00	.18	.50	.50	.50	.50
(6'4") 0.82	.00	.00	.18	.50	.82	.82	.82
(6'8") 0.98	.00	.00	.18	.50	.98	.98	.98
(7'0") 1.00	.00	.00	.18	.50	.98	1.00	1.00

Now, any given premise value of "tall" can be used as a row index in the matrix to extract from the relation the conclusion fuzzy subset representing the possible values of "heavy." The next table shows the conclusion fuzzy subset for a premise value of 6'4".

WEIGHT when HEIGHT is 6′4″

140	0.00
180	0.18
200	0.50
240	0.82
280	0.82
300	0.82

LINGUISTIC VARIABLES IN PRODUCTION RULES

So far we have discussed only fuzzy sets and the relations between them. Real pieces of knowledge are linguistic values of linguistic variables. We say

the price is low

to understand that the linguistic variable "price" takes the linguistic value "low."

A linguistic variable is a *fuzzy variable*, a variable whose value in any one particular instance is a fuzzy subset of a universe of discourse. Consider, for example, the universe of discourse

Dollar : 0   2   4   6   8   10   12

On this universe, we can define the fuzzy subset "low" as follows:

0	1
2	1
4	0.7
6	0.3
8	0.1
10	0
12	0

The base variable of the fuzzy variable is a crisp (nonfuzzy) variable that takes on individual values from the same universe of discourse. Thus, the domain of the base variable is the universe of discourse itself, whereas the domain of the fuzzy variable is the collection of possible fuzzy subsets—"low," "high," "medium"—of this universe of discourse, known as F(Dollar).

A useful way of representing a fuzzy variable is as a vector. The number of dimensions in the vector equals the number of elements in the universe of discourse of the fuzzy variable. The value of each dimension gives the degree to which the corresponding element of the universe of discourse belongs to the fuzzy value of the fuzzy variable. For instance, we can say that "low price" can be represented by the vector

low price: 1   1   0.7   0.3   0.1   0   0

whose elements are the degrees of membership of the fuzzy subset "low."

A *linguistic variable* is a special kind of fuzzy variable distinguished by its association with an appropriate syntax and semantics. The syntax generates a collection of words and phrases to describe all possible fuzzy subsets of the variable's universe of discourse. The semantics provides a unique name from the syntax for any fuzzy value of the variable and a unique fuzzy value for any syntactically correct phrase.

Several synonymous phrases will generate the same fuzzy subset, and several similar fuzzy subsets will generate the same phrase. As a result, the value of a linguistic variable may be given either directly by a fuzzy subset of that variable's universe of discourse or indirectly by a linguistic description. For example, a linguistic variable such as "price" might take the value "low" or the value "more or less medium" as well as a vector representation.

Fuzzy propositions are assertions that the value of a linguistic variable is one particular fuzzy subset in the domain of that variable. That subset is in the set of all fuzzy subsets defined on the variable's universe of discourse.

An example of a fuzzy proposition is

Next month's sales will be better than average.

There are two possible interpretations of the fuzziness of this proposition: either it expresses our uncertainty about what the exact value of next month's sales will be, or it expresses the inherent vagueness of the concept "better than average." This distinction will be discussed when we speak about truth value modification. Compound propositions can be constructed from simple propositions. For this purpose, we can use the three operators AND, OR, and complementation.

A *fuzzy production rule* is a fuzzy relation between two fuzzy propositions. It takes the form

IF proposition 1 THEN proposition 2

This relation defines two functions: generalized *modus ponens* and generalized *modus tollens*.

In the "left-side–driven" or modus ponens mode, the rule com-
pares the data base with proposition 1. If the comparison succeeds,
action is taken in the data base and/or the environment to make the
right-side proposition true. This right-side proposition may be descriptive, such as

Last quarter's average price is above $5

or may be an action proposition, such as

You should charge $6 next quarter.

A computer program embodying a production system does not
have a beginning, a middle, or an end, but only a collection of rules
communicating with each other through the data base. Matching the
left-side proposition with knowledge from the data base is vital for
triggering a production rule. In fuzzy production rules, the concept
"close" is readily defined. If the data come close to matching the left-
side of a particular rule without matching it completely, then the outcome of the rule is somewhat less definite than it would have been if
the match had been better, but the rule is triggered nonetheless.

REPRESENTING KNOWLEDGE BY FUZZY RELATIONS

So far, we have focused on that part of knowledge known as heuristics,
the knowledge embodied in the rules of expertise, the rules of good
practice, the judgmental rules of the field, and the rules of plausible
reasoning. Equally important to the practice of a field are the facts.

A knowledge base surely must contain representations of facts. But
what is a fact? We can agree that a fact is a relationship as well as those
things the relationship ties together in a meaningful way. The following
is a fact:

JOHN LIKES MARY

This simple fact is built of people and tied together by a relationship
with an ordinary name—LIKES. The statement

FRED HAS-HEIGHT 5'7"

is also a fact, but it is built of people and properties tied together by a
relationship with a manufactured name—HAS-HEIGHT. This manu-

factured, hyphenated relation is used whenever the limits of ordinary English make descriptive constellations of words, instead of a single name, necessary. Of course, it is perfectly in order to say that some particular fact is true, very true, not so true, or more or less true.

A particular fact with an internal name TALL can appear in other facts, each perhaps with its own name in turn, for instance

ADRIAN IS TALL

FRED HAS-HEIGHT TALL

Complex knowledge bases are collections of related frames linked together into frame systems. In other words, a knowledge base comprises a network of facts and rules from which new facts can be inferred. In addition, various learning strategies can update these frames with experience.

Again, we can build a vocabulary by representing the meaning of linguistic terms as number arrays. The relational model is a perfect tool for describing facts and their relationships.

The relation

JOHN LIKES MARY

can be defined as a subset of the product space of two domains NAME 1 and NAME 2 from which values JOHN and MARY were selected. We say that the relation LIKES is a subset of the Cartesian product NAME 1 × NAME 2. This definition of the relation can be extended to the fuzzy relation by letting the relation be a fuzzy subset of NAME 1 × NAME 2. For instance, we can say

JOHN LIKES MARY to the degree 0.7

JOHN LIKES MARY to the degree 1.00

In the first case, the tuple (JOHN, MARY) belongs to the relation LIKES to the degree 0.7. The value 0.7 can be interpreted as the tuple's degree of compatibility with the relation. The second case can be interpreted as maximal compatibility, which is assumed in any two-valued logic relational data base.

The fuzzy relation LIKES (NAME 1, NAME 2), where NAME 1 and NAME 2 are attributes, is defined by the mapping

$$f_{\text{LIKES}} : D_1 \times D_2 \rightarrow [0,1]$$

where D_i is the domain of possible values of NAME i and is denoted in table form as depicted below (Baldwin, 1982).

LIKES

NAME 1	NAME 2	Truth Value
JOHN	JILL	0.7
JOHN	MARY	1.0
JACK	FRED	0.6
FRED	HARRY	0.5
HARRY	MARY	0.2
MARY	JOHN	0.9

where $D_1 = D_2 = N = \{$JOHN, HARRY, JACK, MARY, JILL, FRED$\}$. The order of the rows is unimportant. Each row consists of a tuple and a membership degree denoting the level to which the tuple satisfies the relation or is compatible with the relation. Examining the table, we see clearly that John likes Mary more than Jill.

Any crisp relation can be represented as a fuzzy relation if the truth value is specified as 1. For example

PHYSIQUE

NAME	HEIGHT	WEIGHT	Truth Value
JOHN	6'0"	130	1.00
HARRY	5'1"	119	1.00
JACK	5'9"	130	1.00
MARY	5'11"	116	1.00
JILL	5'1"	92	1.00
FRED	5'7"	109	1.00

The definition can be extended so that the elements of the n-tuples can themselves be relations. For instance

PHYSIQUE

NAME	HEIGHT	WEIGHT	Truth Value
JOHN	TALL	HEAVY	1.00
HARRY	5'1"	119	1.00
JACK	NOT TALL	130	1.00
MARY	SHORT	NOT HEAVY	True
JILL	5'1"	92	1.00
FRED	5'7"	NOT HEAVY	0.32

where TALL is defined as

TALL

HEIGHT	Truth Value
5'0"	0.1
5'1"	0.6
5'11"	0.8
6'0"	1.00
7'0"	1.00

We can handle such relations exactly as we handled fuzzy subsets.

Two relations R_1 and R_2 are said to be compatible if and only if they have the same arity (n) and the ith attribute of R_1 and R_2 have the same associated domains (for $i = 1, 2, \ldots, n$). Then, the intersection of R_1 and R_2, denoted R_1 AND R_2, is defined by mapping

$$f_{R_1 \text{ AND } R_2}(t) = \min \left(f_{R_1}(t), f_{R_2}(t) \right)$$

for all the tuples t. The following example illustrates this definition:

R_1

WEIGHT	HEIGHT	Truth Value
w_1	h_1	0.2
w_1	h_2	0.5
w_1	h_3	1.0

R_2

WEIGHT	HEIGHT	Truth Value
w_1	h_2	0.4
w_2	h_2	0.6
w_3	h_2	1.0

$$D_1 = w_1, w_2, w_3$$
$$D_2 = h_1, h_2, h_3$$

R_1 AND R_2

WEIGHT	HEIGHT	Truth Value
w_1	h_2	0.4

The union is obtained using the operator "max." For example

R_1 OR R_2

WEIGHT	HEIGHT	Truth Value
w_1	h_1	0.2
w_1	h_2	0.5
w_1	h_3	1.0
w_2	h_2	0.6
w_3	h_2	1.0

A relation can also be defined as a rule. Such a relation is said to be *virtual*. For example, the rule

$$\text{FRIENDS } (x, y) \leftarrow \text{LIKES } (x, y) \text{ AND LIKES } (y, x)$$

with the base relation LIKES defined above, gives

FRIENDS

NAME 1	NAME 2	Truth Value
JOHN	MARY	0.9
MARY	JOHN	0.9

which by projection onto NAME 1, gives

FRIENDS

NAME	Truth Value
JOHN	0.9
MARY	0.9

The right side of a rule can contain relations that are themselves defined in terms of rules. For instance

PERSON PHYSIQUE (x,y,z) ← IF TALL (x) AND FAT (y) THEN HEAVY (z)
AND
IF SHORT (x) and THIN (y) THEN LIGHT (z)

If we define

IF A THEN B

by

$$f_{\text{IF } A \text{ THEN } B} = \min (f_A, f_B)$$

then we can build another relation whose truth values are given by

$$\min (f_{\text{TALL}}, f_{\text{FAT}}, f_{\text{HEAVY}}, f_{\text{SHORT}}, f_{\text{THIN}}, f_{\text{LIGHT}})$$

These truth values will form the last column in the table

PERSON PHYSIQUE

HEIGHT	DEGREE	WEIGHT	Truth Value

The elements of this table are in fact the elements of the base relations TALL, SHORT, FAT, THIN, HEAVY, LIGHT introduced in the computer as number arrays.

Number arrays from number arrays—this is the philosophy of fuzzy set technology. All these number arrays have names. The user of the knowledge system uses these names. The computer understands the meaning of the names because every name is defined in the vocabulary as a number array.

SUMMARY

1. Knowledge engineering is a discipline dealing with techniques for internalizing (representing and handling) pieces of stored knowledge.
2. Intelligent machines internalize facts, rules, and evaluations.
3. If the system internalizes only facts and rules, the inference mechanism is given by the rules.
4. Rules can be derived automatically from verbal models manipulated by semantic systems.
5. If the system internalizes facts and evaluations, the inference mechanism is given by the logic of evaluations.
6. If the system internalizes facts, rules, and evaluations, the inference mechanism is given by the rules interpreted as relations between fuzzy sets.
7. When knowledge is captured in natural language, linguistic variables are modeled as fuzzy sets, and the internalized logic of fuzzy sets governs evidence combinations.

READINGS

Stefik, M., et al. 1982. The organization of expert systems: a tutorial. *Artificial Intelligence* 18:135–73.

This is a pedagogical tour of cases about the organization of expert problem-solving programs. The tour begins with a restricted class of problems that admits a very simple organization. To be feasible, the organization requires that the input data be static and reliable and that the solution space be small enough to allow an exhaustive search. These assumptions are then relaxed, one at a time, in case studies of ten more sophisticated organizational prescriptions. Ways to cope with unreliable data or knowledge are considered. Probabilistic, fuzzy, and exact methods are discussed.

All of these methods are based on the idea of increasing reliability by combining evidence. Each method requires the use of metaknowledge about how to combine evidence. The fuzzy approaches use fuzzy set descriptions, the probabilistic approaches use prior and conditional estimates, and the exact approaches use nonmonotonic data correction rules. Ways to work with time-varying data are considered, with the conclusion that ways to reason with time seem to require more research. The remaining cases deal with ways to cope with large search spaces.

Research on expert systems has benefited from the simplicity of using uniform representation systems. However, as knowledge bases get larger, the efficiency penalty incurred by using declarative and uniform representations can become significant. Attention to these matters will become increasingly important in ambitiously conceived future expert systems with increasingly large knowledge bases.

Architectural approaches for tuning the performance of expert systems by making changes to the representation of knowledge are now available. Three main ideas are considered: use of specialized data structures, knowledge compilation, and knowledge transformations for cognitive economy. By compilation, one means any process that transforms one representation of knowledge into another representation which can be used more efficiently. The techniques for such transformations are just beginning to be explored and will probably become increasingly important in the next few years. The term *cognitive economy* refers to systems that automatically improve their performance by changing representations.

Whalen, T., and Schott, B. 1983. Decision support with fuzzy production systems. In *Advances in fuzzy sets, possibility theory, and applications*, ed. P. Wang. Decision Sciences Laboratory, Georgia State University, Atlanta. New York: Plenum.

A computer program embodying a production system does not have a beginning, a middle, or an end, but only a collection of rules communicating with each other through the data base. This structure makes the overall execution sequence of a production system extremely difficult to predict in advance despite the simplicity of the microlevel behavior and the readability of the postexecution trace. A production system is neither truly sequential nor truly parallel from a programming point of view because the execution of one production rule changes the data base that determines which production rule is executed next.

Closely related to this difficulty is the problem of conflict resolution, which occurs when the contents of the data base match the left side of more than one rule at some particular point in processing. In such a case, the effect on the data base is different depending on which rule is executed first. Most successful programs using the production system structure resolve this problem by adding a procedurally coded executive routine or else by using nonintuitive housekeeping rules to maintain various switches and flags in the data base. Because these mechanisms have no real-world significance, they are not meaningful to the expert who provides the basic rules.

Classical production systems are rooted in a two-valued logic, and thus production rules must be executed in an all-or-nothing manner. Rules are executed if the pattern of their left-side proposition matches a pattern found in the data base; otherwise, rules are not executed. In effect, all variables are treated as if they were measurable only on nominal scales. For a classical production system to make use of a variable measured on a numeric scale, the scale must be divided into regions, and production rules whose left sides ask whether the variable is located in a given region must be written. In other words, there is no concept of "closeness."

The fuzzy production systems methodology described in this paper takes a radical approach to these disadvantages by examining the potential for building a new kind of production system on a framework of fuzzy logic. A production rule is viewed as a fuzzy implication, that is, a fuzzy relation between two fuzzy propositions. Over half a dozen definitions of fuzzy implication have been put forth. They differ in the details whereby propositions interact. A detailed discussion of these definitions can be found in Whalen and Schott, below.

Whalen, T., and Schott, B. 1981. Issues in fuzzy production systems. Paper presented at the 1st Annual Conference of North American Fuzzy Information Processing (NAFIP), May 1981, at University of Utah, Logan. Published in *International Journal of Man-Machine Studies* 19 (1983) 57–71.

The purpose of this study is to examine some critical issues in the development of practical knowledge-based systems using fuzzy logic and related techniques. The authors survey eight current and proposed implementations of such systems to provide a context for examining the following three general topics: the representation of the implication (IF-THEN) operator, the nature and locus of uncertainty, and the method and role of data base updating and system dynamics in the system. The goal was not to determine which treatment of these issues is best overall, but rather to draw on current practical experience to begin mapping the advantages and disadvantages of each option relative to the specific structure of the application addressed.

Wenstop, F. 1980. Quantitative analysis with linguistic values. *Fuzzy Sets and Systems* 4:99–115.

The concept of quantitative analysis of verbal models is set out and discussed. Wenstop presents an APL-implemented auxiliary language that makes quantitative analysis operational in humanistic systems using variables that cannot be measured numerically with ease. The quasinatural auxiliary language with deductive properties is constructed after general fuzzy set theoretic principles. This language imposes an important restriction on the type of attribute to be used in the model. The meanings of all linguistic values are modeled independently of context and with respect to a psychological continuum representing the range of an attribute on an interval scale. For this reason, the language is useful primarily for those attributes, such as attitudes, that lack a natural objective scale. Examples are level of bureaucracy, innovation, depth of love, and so on. Examples of attributes with objective scales are age, organization size, profit, and so on. The auxiliary language is probably too coarse for objective attributes because finer shades of meaning with respect to quantities should be expressible under such circumstances.

It is sometimes maintained that using fuzzy sets to model inexactness is somehow like cheating because fuzzy set models are just as exact as corresponding numeric models. One succeeds only in introducing a large number of extraneous assumptions. This is not true. Wenstop demonstrates that the auxiliary language is robust against changes in its semantic foundation as long as these do not violate common-sense principles. More precisely, the author tries several different shapes for the meaning of the primary terms, and the effect is insignificant. He also substitutes the min-max operators, and the characteristics do not change appreciably.

Baldwin, J. F. 1982. An automated fuzzy reasoning algorithm. In *Fuzzy set and possibility theory*, ed. R. Yager. New York: Pergamon Press.

Baldwin presents a reasoning algorithm based on a fuzzy logic of truth value restrictions. The algorithm is to be used with a fuzzy knowledge base. The knowledge base is a set of fuzzy propositions applicable to an object set. For example, a medical dictionary is applicable to the set of human beings.

This paper distinguishes between fuzzy reasoning and approximate reasoning. Fuzzy reasoning is simply reasoning according to fuzzy logic of truth value restrictions and is in no way approximate. Fuzzy reasoning does allow for the inclusion of vague statements and could therefore be described as vague reasoning. Vague reasoning uses a precise method of analysis according to the theory of fuzzy subsets where only the membership is relaxed. Approximate reasoning occurs when the precise method of analysis used in fuzzy reasoning is approximated in some sense. This approximation is necessary to avoid high-dimensional computation. By this definition, approximate reasoning amounts to relaxing the condition of equality.

A language suitable for use with the algorithm is described. It is of a list type and is easily processed in LISP, which is used for development purposes. The knowledge base is in the form of lists of information structures associated with property names of property lists and universal sets.

Baldwin, J. F., and Zhou, S. Q. 1982. A fuzzy relational inference language. *EM/FS Research Report*. Dept. of Engineering Mathematics, University of Bristol, England.

A general query language, which uses fuzzy base relations and rewriting rules, is described. The language can be viewed as a high-level automatic inference knowledge-based system similar to PROLOG but based on the mathematics of relations instead of predicate calculus and incorporating a fuzzy inference capability through fuzzy relations. The user provides a knowledge base of facts and rules from which queries can be answered automatically. The automation of the inference process is not of the search or resolution variety associated with theorem-proving in artificial intelligence but rather analogous to Gaussian elimination for the solution of linear equations. The knowledge base is in the form of base relations and rules for determining virtual relations. More details about fuzzy relational data bases can be found in Prade and Testemale, Umano, Sack et al., and Buckles and Petry, below.

Prade, H., and Testemale, C. 1983. Generalizing data base relational algebra for treatment of incomplete/uncertain information and vague queries. Paper presented at the 2d Annual Conference of North American Fuzzy Information Processing (NAFIP), June 1983, at Schenectady, New York. Available as a report from University Paul Sabatier, Toulouse, France.

Umano, M. 1982. FREEDOM-O: a fuzzy database system. In *Fuzzy information and decision processes*, eds. M. Gupta and E. Sanchez. Amsterdam: North Holland.

Implemented in FORTRAN.

Sack, I. H., Giardina, C., and Sinha, D. 1983. Investigations into fuzzy relational databases. Paper presented at the 2d Annual Conference of North American Fuzzy Information Processing (NAFIP), June 1983, at Schenectady, New York. Available as Report 8315, Stevens Institute of Technology, Hoboken, New Jersey.

The author presents a fuzzy relational data base query program written in the C programming language.

Buckles, B., and Petry, F. 1982. Fuzzy databases and their applications. In *Fuzzy information and decision processes*, eds. M. Gupta and E. Sanchez. Amsterdam: North-Holland.

Buckles, B., and Petry, F. 1983. Extension of the fuzzy database with fuzzy arithmetic. Paper presented at the 2d Annual Conference of North American Fuzzy Information Processing (NAFIP), June 1983, at Schenectady, New York.

The fuzzy relational data base model originated by the authors permits fuzzy domain values from a discrete, finite universe. Buckles and Petry extend the model by demonstrating that fuzzy numbers may be employed as domain values without loss of consistency with respect to representation or the relational algebra. Where equivalence is required in an ordinary relational data base, similarity is employed in a fuzzy relational data base. For discrete, finite universes, similarity between atomic elements is described via a fuzzy similarity relation with max-min transitivity. Two or more fuzzy numbers are defined as similar if their union forms a continuous level set over the real line. This convention effects the partitioning of fuzzy number domains, thus ensuring that the fuzzy relational algebra is well-defined.

CHAPTER FIVE

Approximate Reasoning

This chapter introduces a new field, which has come to be called approximate reasoning. Although approximate reasoning is concerned with both the means for representing natural language propositions into a machine-understandable form and the methodology for making inferences from this information, in principle the representation is separable from the inference procedure.

A knowledge-based system consists of only two things: a knowledge base and an inference procedure. The knowledge base consists of facts (and rules). The inference procedure consists of processes applied to the knowledge base.

The act of obtaining and formalizing the facts and the rules is called "expertise modeling." The goal of inference procedures is to permit the computer to write a program. In contrast to ordinary situations, no programmer comes between the user and the computer. The user specifies a problem, and the computer is smart enough to "understand" and solve it.

Building smart computers means endowing them with reasoning capabilities and knowledge. According to the theory of approximate reasoning, the result of applying rules of inference to natural language statements translated into fuzzy sets is other fuzzy sets. The resulting fuzzy sets, upon retranslation, lead to approximate consequents of the original premises.

RULES OF INFERENCE

A principal conclusion of the previous chapter on knowledge representation is that before a computer can deal with a sentence, the sentence must be translated into an internal description that captures its meaning. We will look now at what it is possible to do in the context of such a representation.

We have seen that the proposition

JOHN IS TALL

can be represented as a vector or a table, depending on how the linguistic value TALL is represented. This is true because the linguistic variable JOHN is substituted by the linguistic value TALL. We can say that the proposition has the effect of limiting the values JOHN may assume to the *possibility distribution* identified with TALL.

No matter what we say, the fact is that the proposition JOHN IS TALL is represented as a number array. This number array is a table defining the fuzzy subset TALL on the set "heights."

Assume now that there is a known correspondence between the set HEIGHTS and the set WEIGHTS. In this context, "known" means that this correspondence has a machine representation—it is in the computer, as another table

HEIGHTS	WEIGHTS
5′0″	100
5′4″	140
5′8″	160
6′0″	200
6′4″	240
6′8″	280
7′0″	300

Due to this correspondence, a fuzzy subset TALL defined on HEIGHTS will induce a fuzzy subset on WEIGHTS such that we can speak about a *natural inference*. We can call this second fuzzy subset HEAVY.

Now, consider that we are not able to swear that such a function exists—that we cannot specify the correspondence exactly. In real life this is the case. What we do have, however, is a fuzzy relation; for instance, the table

HEIGHTS	WEIGHTS	Truth Value
5'0"	100	0.8
5'4"	140	0.9
5'8"	160	0.7
6'0"	200	0.5
6'4"	240	0.6
6'8"	280	0.4
7'0"	300	0.3

Due to this new correspondence, a fuzzy subset TALL defined on HEIGHTS will induce another fuzzy subset on WEIGHTS, but in this case, we have a *compositional inference*. That means that the membership degrees of the new fuzzy subset induced by TALL will differ from the membership degrees of TALL. They will result from the composition of the membership in TALL and the membership in the relation HEIGHTS-WEIGHTS.

It cannot be more true that an element is in the induced fuzzy subset than it is true that it is either in TALL or in the relation linking HEIGHTS with WEIGHTS. Therefore, if

$$TALL : HEIGHTS \rightarrow [0,1]$$
$$RELATION: HEIGHTS \times WEIGHTS \rightarrow [0,1]$$

the membership function of the new fuzzy subset induced on WEIGHTS will be

$$f(\text{weight}) = \max_{\text{heights}} \min (f_{TALL}(\text{height}), f_{RELATION})$$

This is equivalent to taking the *projection* of the RELATION onto HEIGHTS, denoted by

$$\text{Proj}_{HEIGHTS} RELATION = \max_{\text{heights}} f_{RELATION}(h, w)$$

and intersected with TALL, which is defined on the same carrier (domain) HEIGHTS.

An important application of this rule is to information of the following type:

$$JOHN \ IS \ TALL$$
$$IF \ JOHN \ IS \ SHORT \ THEN \ BIKE \ IS \ SMALL$$

Using the rule of compositional inference, we can infer a value for BIKE.

We can go a step further and speak about the composition of two fuzzy relations. Consider two relations R_1 and R_2 as given in the tables

R_1

HEIGHTS	WEIGHTS	Truth Value
5'0"	100	0.8
5'8"	160	0.7
6'4"	240	0.6
7'0"	300	1.0

R_2

WEIGHTS	PRICE	Truth Value
100	YELLOW	0.2
160	RED	0.6
240	GREY	0.8
300	GREY	0.9

From the relation R_1, we see that the height of 5'8" and the weight 160 are related to the degree 0.7. From the relation R_2, we can see that the weight 160 is related to the price RED to the degree 0.6. Therefore, we have no reason to believe that the height of 5'8" is linked with the price RED to a degree greater than 0.6. For this reason, the composition of these two relations, denoted R_{12} is given by selecting the minimal values for membership, according to the rule

$$f_{R_{12}}(\text{height, price}) = \max_{\text{weights}} \min (f_{R_1}(h, w), f_{R_2}(w, p))$$

An important application of this rule is to knowledge of the following type:

IF JOHN IS TALL THEN THE BIKE IS BIG
IF THE BIKE IS BIG THEN ITS PRICE IS UNACCEPTABLE

Using the rule of composition for relations, we can infer

IF JOHN IS SMALL THEN THE BIKE PRICE IS ACCEPTABLE

WHAT IS TRUTH? COMPATIBILITY

The truth variable plays a considerable role in the theory of approximate reasoning. We say

JOHN IS TALL

to assert conformity with facts or reality. In fact, what we want to say is

JOHN IS TALL is true

or according to our linguistic variable approach

the truth is that JOHN IS TALL

But people often say

JOHN IS TALL is very true
JOHN IS TALL is more or less true
JOHN IS TALL is not so true

What does this mean? Well, it seems that the linguistic variable "truth" has more than one linguistic value. How can we take this reality into account; in other words, how can we represent this fact?

If we examine the linguistic values *true, very true,* and *more or less true,* we see that they are differentiated by the modifiers *very* and *more or less.* In the chapter devoted to knowledge representation, we saw that we can define "very tall" by starting with the fuzzy subset TALL and modifying the membership degrees by contraction. If we want to follow this example, then we have to represent "true" as a fuzzy subset. We can do that by considering "true" as a fuzzy subset of the unit interval

$$\text{true}: [0,1] \rightarrow [0,1]$$

In this way, the concept of truth serves in the main as a mechanism for assessing the *compatibility* of a pair of propositions.

Consider the table

True	
0.0	0.0
0.2	0.2
0.5	0.5
0.7	0.7
0.9	0.9
1.0	1.0

We can derive "very true" from this table simply by modifying the column containing the degrees of membership

Very True	
0.0	0.0
0.2	0.04
0.5	0.25
0.7	0.49
0.9	0.81
1.0	1.0

Now that we know the meaning of "very true," we can understand the meaning of the proposition

JOHN IS TALL is very true

This is the meaning of a new proposition

JOHN IS somehow

where SOMEHOW is a fuzzy subset *related* to TALL. We say that TALL induces "somehow" via "very true," and express the relation as

$$f_{somehow} = \min \left(f_{very\ true}, f_{TALL} \right)$$

It cannot be more true that an element is in the induced fuzzy subset than it is true that it is either in TALL or in very true.

KNOWLEDGE DIAGRAMS ARE MODELS OF FUZZY SYSTEMS

The reader should not be surprised at the use of the word *induce* to explain how fuzzy subsets can be used to infer by reasoning from particular facts. The usual definition of *inference* is to discover by reasoning, and we added only a realistic assumption, that of approximate reasoning.

Does this mean that computational theories of approximate reasoning hold promise as models of human reasoning? The answer is yes, at least to those researchers of human systems who use the same metaphors as researchers dedicated to making computers smarter.

Knowledge diagrams, for example, help us understand how smart systems can simulate the behavior of human systems. The idea of a knowledge diagram is not merely natural, it is forced on us by the structure of fuzzy objects if we admit, as I think we must, that the lattice criterion for union is right. In other words, if we admit that we can use the min operator to intersect two fuzzy subsets, the algebraic structure of fuzzy sets is evident.

The idea of a knowledge diagram is natural because each time a human system acquires intelligence, that person's state of knowledge changes—a movement takes place in that person's structure of images, a kind of regression toward a terminal in this structure. The theory of fuzzy systems tries to formalize this structure.

By *diagram*, we simply mean a display of objects linked by arrows. For example

$$\text{FRIENDS } (x, y) \rightarrow \text{LIKES } (x, y)$$

is a diagram between two relations

FRIENDS			LIKES		
NAME 1	NAME 2	Truth	NAME 1	NAME 2	Truth
JOHN	MARY	0.9	JOHN	JILL	0.7
MARY	JOHN	0.9	JOHN	MARY	1.0
			JACK	FRED	0.6
			FRED	HARRY	0.5
			HARRY	MARY	0.2
			MARY	JOHN	0.9

FRIENDS (x, y), as a fuzzy relation, is included in LIKES (x, y), and the rule "an element of FRIENDS (x, y) is an element of LIKES (x, y)" provides a function. In this case, we speak about the inclusion function. The word *inclusion* indicates an action. The function *acts* to include the elements of FRIENDS (x, y) among those of LIKES (x, y). However, the word *function* presents a difficulty. The identity function on FRIENDS (x, y) and the inclusion function from FRIENDS (x, y) to LIKES (x, y) are conceptually quite different, as set-theoretical entities, but are identical physically—they are exactly the same set of ordered pairs.

An arrow is a primary perspective abstracted from a function or a mapping. The idea is to define properties of a collection by reference to its external relationships with other collections instead of by reference to its internal structure. Several standard diagrams can be formulated in the language of arrows. The basic idea is the *cone*. A cone of a diagram consists of a new object and new arrows. For instance, consider this arrowless diagram.

LIKES (x, y) LIKES (y, x)

Its cone could be the diagram

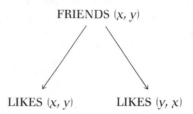

A *limit* is a cone with the property that exactly one arrow links it to another cone. For instance, if we define LOVERS (x, y) as FRIENDS (x, y) with a degree of relation greater than 0.8, we have the diagram

LOVERS $(x, y) \rightarrow$ FRIENDS (x, y)

such that

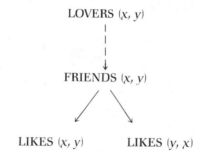

The limiting cone, when it exists, is universal among such cones. Any other cone factors uniquely, a factoring represented by a dashed arrow in the last diagram.

A *pullback* of a pair of arrows with a common codomain is a *limit* for this diagram. In the previous example both LIKES (x, y) and LIKES (y, x) can be included in the relation UNKNOWN, which means that the intensity or degree of membership of the affection is not known. We know, however, that the pair exists. Therefore, UNKNOWN is a relation in which all degrees of membership are equal to 1. If so, FRIENDS (x, y) is the pullback of LIKES (x, y) and LIKES (y, x). We can say that FRIENDS (x, y) arrives by pulling back LIKES $(x, y) \rightarrow$ UNKNOWN along LIKES $(y, x) \rightarrow$ UNKNOWN.

The pullback is a fundamental notion in the algebraic approach taken in approximate reasoning toward the concept of compatibility. *Truth*, in approximate reasoning, is mainly a mechanism for assessing the compatibility of a pair of propositions rather than, as in classical logic, an indicator of the correspondence between a proposition and reality.

The following examples, illustrating the pullback's working and generality, are worthy of detailed examination.

Example 1.   The pullback

$$
\begin{array}{ccc}
\text{true} & \xrightarrow{\;f'\;} & \text{TALL} \\
{\scriptstyle g'}\big\downarrow & & \big\downarrow{\scriptstyle g} \\
\text{TALL} & \xrightarrow[\;f\;]{} & \text{UNKNOWN}
\end{array}
$$

of two functions f and g is defined by

$$\text{true} = \{(x, y), \text{TALL}: X \rightarrow [0,1] \; x \in X, y \in X \text{ and } f(x) = g(y)\}$$

with

$$f'(x, y) = y$$
$$g'(x, y) = x$$

"True," then is a subset of the product set TALL $\times$ TALL; that is, a fuzzy set of the unit interval.

Example 2.   If $f{:}\text{TALL} \rightarrow \text{HEAVY}$ is a function, and VERY HEAVY is a subset of HEAVY, then the inverse image of VERY HEAVY under f, denoted $f^{-1}(\text{VERY HEAVY})$, is the subset of TALL consisting of all the f-inputs whose corresponding outputs lie in VERY HEAVY.

The diagram

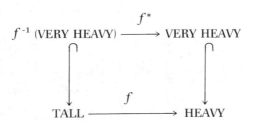

is a pullback square, where the curved arrows denote inclusions, and $f^*(x) = f(x)$ for x in f^{-1} (VERY HEAVY); that is, f^* is a restriction of f to

f^{-1}(VERY HEAVY). Thus, the inverse image of VERY HEAVY under f arises by pulling VERY HEAVY back along f.

Example 3.   Assume the knowledge base

TALL
PERSON
LIKES

and a question

Who likes a tall person?

We can build the following diagram

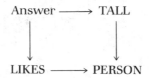

For instance (Baldwin, 1982)

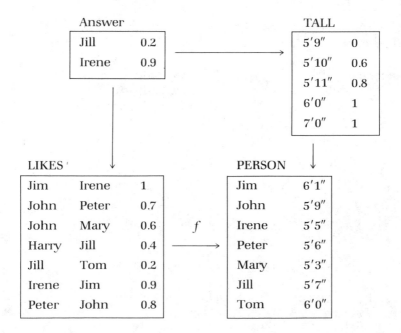

The answer is the subset of LIKES consisting of all the *f*-inputs whose corresponding outputs lie in PERSON. The inverse image of PERSON arises by pulling TALL back along *f*.

TRUTH QUESTIONS

We have seen in a previous section that a proposition

JOHN IS TALL is more or less true

is equivalent to another proposition

JOHN IS SOMEHOW

where SOMEHOW is a fuzzy subset induced by the fuzzy subset TALL. In other words, the compatibility of TALL and SOMEHOW is given by the fuzzy subset "more or less true." We have seen further that the proposition JOHN IS TALL pulled back along another proposition JOHN IS SOMEHOW means "more or less true."

Bearing these facts in mind, we can understand why a knowledge system whose knowledge base includes the proposition JOHN IS SHORT will answer "not true" when the question IS JOHN TALL? is posed. The answer of the system is the compatibility of TALL, the question, with SHORT, the knowledge. Both are defined on the same domain, the set of heights.

In this situation, there is only one source of knowledge about JOHN and the answer is arrived at by comparing this unique source with the question. Both the knowledge and the question are simple base representations—fuzzy propositions. First, the system constructs a knowledge tree from the knowledge and the question items. The tree is easily completed because all the branches, in this case two, terminate in base representations. The evaluation procedure reduces the tree, according to a pullback diagram

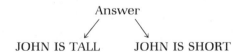

The derivation of the knowledge tree about JOHN is a forward process, while the evaluation is a backward contraction, a pullback in the structure of descriptors.

Practically, the system's answer is a fuzzy subset of the unit interval; that is, a table whose columns represent the degrees of membership in one of the descriptors. If the two descriptors are represented as in the following table

TALL		SHORT	
HEIGHTS	Truth Value	HEIGHTS	Truth Value
5'0"	0.00	5'0"	1.00
5'4"	0.08	5'4"	0.92
5'8"	0.32	5'8"	0.68
6'0"	0.50	6'0"	0.50
6'4"	0.82	6'4"	0.18
6'8"	0.98	6'8"	0.02
7'0"	1.00	7'0"	0.00

then the answer is the fuzzy subset

Answer	
0.00	1.00
0.08	0.92
0.32	0.68
0.50	0.50
0.82	0.18
0.98	0.02
1.00	0.00

This is precisely the negation of "true," the fuzzy subset of the unit interval whose table is

True	
0.00	0.00
0.08	0.08
0.32	0.32
0.50	0.50
0.82	0.82
0.98	0.98
1.00	1.00

From this table we can *induce* "very true" simply by squaring the second column and "fairly true" by taking the square root.

Other tables can be labeled in a variety of other situations when the second column does not take standard forms of the referent "true."

If we wish to create a complete semantic system, it is not enough to devise rules for computation and representation of meaning. We also have to design rules for an opposite purpose—to assign appropriate linguistic labels to a given meaning. A meaning representation system is a function from the set of linguistic values to the set of fuzzy subsets. A linguistic approximation routine is a function from the set of fuzzy subsets to a set of linguistic values.

This is so because in the fuzzy set approach, knowledge engineering means more than symbolic manipulation and symbolic inference. It also means computation, if one admits that handling number arrays is computation.

VALUE QUESTIONS

In the previous section, we interrogated a knowledge system whose knowledge base was very poor. The base contained only one knowledge item, and that item was represented as a simple proposition. In the construction of real expert systems, the most important problem is to make inferences from large knowledge bases. The power of an expert system resides in the size of its knowledge base.

The type of knowledge we shall initially consider is made up of propositions and production rules. The problem is to use the theory of approximate reasoning to obtain some desired knowledge from the knowledge base.

An important type of inquiry centers on finding the value of a variable about which the knowledge base has some details. We can begin with the question

How is John?

Some examples shed light on how the theory of approximate reasoning helps us find knowledge when we face such a question. Assume a knowledge base consisting of three propositions

JOHN IS TALL
MARY IS BEAUTIFUL
JOHN IS INTELLIGENT

Let us call any basic proposition using JOHN, the variable in the query, a *descriptor* or a *partial value*. The complete value of the variable JOHN is obtained by conjunction of partial values. In this case, the complete value of JOHN is

TALL AND INTELLIGENT

When we ask the knowledge base the value of the variable, it generates a knowledge tree about the variable.

Answer

JOHN IS TALL   JOHN IS INTELLIGENT

The evaluation reduces the tree. The derivation of the knowledge tree is a forward process, while its evaluation is a backward contraction process, a pullback in the structure of descriptions.

In the next case, we shall assume a knowledge base consisting of three propositions and a production rule.

JOHN IS TALL
MARY IS BEAUTIFUL
JOHN IS INTELLIGENT
IF MARY IS VERY BEAUTIFUL THEN JOHN IS VERY ATTENTIVE

We have now three sources of partial knowledge about JOHN, and complete knowledge again can be obtained by conjunction. However, the partial knowledge contained in the production rule is not readily amenable to conjunction. We shall first apply the rule of compositional inference to the second proposition and the production rule. The resulting fuzzy subset is retranslated into a proposition by linguistic approximation. This is so because TALL and INTELLIGENT and ATTENTIVE are not defined on the same domain (universe of discourse). Therefore we obtain the third partial value of JOHN by computation, and then aggregate all the values by symbolic manipulation.

If instead of INTELLIGENT we had another fuzzy subset also defined on heights, as TALL is, then we might derive the intersection from JOHN IS TALL and the third proposition. This is the case of the following knowledge base (Bonissone, 1982).

JOHN IS VERY TALL IS RATHER FALSE
JOHN IS TALLER THAN PAOLA
MARY IS TALLER THAN PAOLA IS FALSE
MARY IS TALLER THAN ANN
PAOLA IS OF MEDIUM HEIGHT
ANN IS VERY SHORT
NANCY IS MUCH TALLER THAN ANN
GAIL IS INDEED VERY TALL
NANCY IS NOT MUCH SHORTER THAN GAIL
DENNIS IS SHORTER THAN JOHN
DENNIS IS TALLER THAN MARY

Suppose we ask HOW IS DENNIS? We can obtain the answer by taking the intersection (via the operator AND) of the assignments associated with the linguistic variable DENNIS. This procedure is purely syntactical. The answer, after symbolic manipulation alone, is long and almost incomprehensible.

> DENNIS IS SHORTER THAN VERY TALL IS RATHER FALSE
> AND TALLER THAN MEDIUM HEIGHT
> AND TALLER THAN TALLER THAN VERY SHORT
> AND TALLER THAN MEDIUM HEIGHT IS FALSE

At this point, linguistic approximation is used to simplify the answer. The meaning of each answer is determined by obtaining the corresponding membership distribution, and a more understandable label is associated with it. For our knowledge base, the answers are

> JOHN IS SORT OF TALL
> DENNIS IS BETWEEN MEDIUM HEIGHT AND RATHER TALL
> MARY IS FROM SORT OF SHORT TO MEDIUM HEIGHT
> NANCY IS VERY TALL

It is important to note that the obtained answers are not precise, since they do not specify height in meters or feet. On the contrary, they reflect the fuzziness of the input data. Nevertheless, the answers are perfectly consistent with the ones provided by a human using intuitive understanding of the data and approximate reasoning.

VARIABLE QUESTIONS

Real-life knowledge bases are very complex. They are built of propositions, production rules, and frames that, together, capture the knowledge of the field as data structures in the memory of the computer. These structures can be conveniently accessed to answer difficult questions. How is this knowledge used to answer questions? Essentially, the design of the inference engine hinges on this question. How many inference engine designs are available? Many, but here we shall discuss a relational inference language called FRIL (an acronym for Fuzzy Relational Inference Language, exactly as APL is an acronym for A Programming Language).

Assume a knowledge base with the following content (Baldwin, 1982):

IF LIKES (NAME 1, NAME 2) AND LIKES (NAME 2, NAME 1)
THEN FRIENDS (NAME 1, NAME 2)

LIKES (NAME 1, NAME 2)

PERSON (NAME, HEIGHT, WEIGHT)

TALL (HEIGHT)

In this base, PERSON, LIKES, and TALL are tables.
   In response to the question

WHO LIKES A TALL PERSON?

the system returns

LIKES (NAME 1, NAME 2)
AND
PERSON (NAME, HEIGHT)
AND
TALL (HEIGHT)

This is a reduction tree structure of relations.

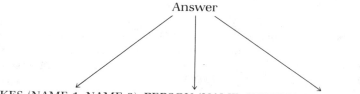

Answer

LIKES (NAME 1, NAME 2) PERSON (NAME, HEIGHT) TALL (HEIGHT)

The reduction process eliminates variables one at a time to produce a succession of reduction trees until the answer is obtained. The basic idea is that the argument of the answer is taken directly from the first argument of LIKES. The variable HEIGHT is eliminated by the composition of the two relations PERSON and TALL. The variable NAME 2 is then eliminated by the composition of the result with LIKES. The system is simply contracting backward by pullback in the structure of relations starting with base relations, that is, with facts. During this process, if the question does not use base relations, a production rule is processed. For instance, in response to the question

WHO ARE FRIENDS?

the system returns

LIKES (NAME 1, NAME 2)
AND
LIKES (NAME 1, NAME 2)

This is a tree structure of the base relations.

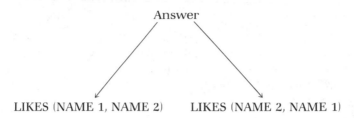

Again, when a question is posed, (for instance, the name of a variable) the knowledge base generates a knowledge tree and reduces the tree during evaluation. The derivation of the knowledge tree is a forward process, and the evaluation is a backward contraction, a pullback in the structure of the frames.

SUMMARY

1. In the fuzzy set approach, the rules of inference can be derived from the rules of representation. In fact, they are a consequence of the rules of representation.

2. Adopting the fuzzy set approach to knowledge representation means transforming any proposition in a function with values into an evaluation lattice (usually the unit interval), that is, an order structure.

3. In general terms, a structure includes some constants and operations (for instance, the constant of the lowest limit, the less-than-or-equal-operation, and zero) and is subject to some laws (for instance, the commutative and associative laws). Any structured collection of objects is closed under such a set of transformations. In other words, we can use an operation to obtain each object from other objects in the same collection.

4. A useful feature of this abstraction is that an evaluation and the set of all evaluations have the same structure. The aim of the theory of fuzzy systems is to exploit this fact.

5. Knowledge trees can be seen as paths in the set of all evaluations. Each node-proposition is obtained from other node-propositions through an operation.

6. The evaluation of a knowledge tree means synthesis of partial evaluations, node by node, starting at the root. Reduction is a pullback toward a constant of the structure.

7. Multiple evaluations are associated with undecidability generated by conflict, which is easily described by a dialectical logic, that is, a logic not governed by the principle of the excluded middle.

8. It is the contention of this book that further progress in the foundations of knowledge engineering will depend largely on the understanding of certain natural structures, whose unifying role has recently become increasingly apparent. The key idea is that of a category of fuzzy sets.

9. If we consider functions between fuzzy sets defined on different universes of discourse, then the constructions of the category of fuzzy sets are rules of inference.

10. A display of fuzzy sets and the functions between them is a diagram. A display of propositions and the functions between them is a knowledge diagram.

11. The rules of inference can be described in knowledge diagrams, and knowledge tree theory can be formulated in a simple categorial language.

12. If a rational inference is one drawn from an established or widely accepted theory, then approximate reasoning is rational.

READINGS

Zadeh, L. A. 1978. Fuzzy sets as a basis for a theory of possibility. *Fuzzy Sets and Systems* 1:3–28.

Zadeh's is the classic text on approximate reasoning and introduces the concept of possibility distribution as a fuzzy constraint. If F is a fuzzy subset of X, then the proposition "Y is F" induces a possibility distribution. $P_Y = F$. We say that the proposition "Y is F" has the effect of constraining the values Y may assume, with the possibility distribution P_Y identified with F. In this framework, the rules for modifiers, quantification, truth qualification, and conjunction can be systematized easily. The compositional rule of inference, which includes the classical *modus ponens* as a special case, can be obtained by combining the projection and conjunction rules.

Zadeh, L. A. 1983. *A theory of common-sense knowledge.* Memorandum No. UCB/ERL M83/26 (17 April 1983), Electronics Research Laboratory, College of Engineering, University of California, Berkeley.

Zadeh outlines a theory based on the idea that what is called common-sense knowledge may be viewed as a collection of *dis-*

positions, that is, propositions with implied fuzzy quantifiers. In this sense, the proposition "Tall men are not very agile" is a disposition that, upon restoration, is converted into the proposition "Most tall men are not very agile." In this proposition, *most* is an explicit fuzzy quantifier that approximately characterizes the proposition "men who are not very agile" among "men who are tall." Traditional logic provides no ways to represent the meaning of propositions with fuzzy quantifiers, and Zadeh suggests that fuzzy logic provides an appropriate computational framework.

As its name implies, fuzzy logic is the logic of approximate reasoning. Fuzzy logic has two principal components: meaning representation and meaning inference. The first component is, in effect, a translation system for representing meaning. The term *test-score semantics* is employed to refer to this translation system because it involves an aggregation of the test scores of elastic constraints induced by the semantic entity whose meaning is represented. Inference from dispositions may be viewed as an alternative to default reasoning and nonmonotonic logic. Fuzzy logic provides a computational framework for dealing with common-sense knowledge. This framework is of great relevance to the management of uncertainty in expert systems. The advantage of employing fuzzy logic in expert systems is that it provides a systematic framework for syllogistic reasoning and thus puts the derivation of combining functions for uncertain evidence on a firmer basis.

Yager, R. 1982. *Querying knowledge base systems with linguistic information via knowledge trees.* Tech. Report MII-204, Machine Intelligence Institute, Iona College, New Rochelle, New York.

Yager develops an approach to querying knowledge systems containing linguistic data and linguistic implicational statements. Yager uses the theory of possibility to provide a calculus to represent and reason with imprecise information found in linguistic knowledge bases. An algorithmic procedure consisting of the development of a knowledge tree and an evaluation procedure is presented.

Yager, R. 1982. *Knowledge trees on complex knowledge bases.* Tech. Report MII-209. Machine Intelligence Institute, Iona College, New Rochelle, New York.

In this paper, Yager extends his ideas to allow (1) the inclusion of relational propositions in the knowledge base and (2) more complicated queries to the knowledge base.

Yager, R. 1982. Binary answers to imprecise questions. *Kybernetes* 11:285–95.

This is an excellent discussion of the problem of answering truth questions. In many real-life situations, people are asked imprecise questions, have imprecise information, yet have to give a yes or no answer, for example, the "guilty or not guilty" courtroom verdict. The analogy between answering questions and making decisions at junction points is readily seen. There is a close connection between approximate reasoning and algorithm building because many of the steps of an algorithm imply logical manipulation of imprecise questions.

The next three readings describe work done in FRIL, a fuzzy relational inference language developed at the Department of Engineering Mathematics, University of Bristol, England.

Baldwin, J. F. 1982. Knowledge engineering using a fuzzy relational inference language. *Report EM/FS*.

Knowledge bases contain base relations, virtual relations, set theoretic relations, and functions. *Base* relations are tables of facts whose tuples (rows of the table) to some degree satisfy the relation, which takes on values in the unit interval and represents a fuzzy truth value. Each column is associated with an attribute that can take values from an associated domain. A relation can also be defined as a rewrite rule containing other relations and constructs of FRIL. Such a relation is said to be *virtual*. The logical connectives AND, OR, NOT, and their fuzzy logic equivalents can be used to define virtual relations. The user asks questions through the query language provided by the system. The user input is passed to a processor, which separates multiple queries into single-command queries. Single-command queries are translated into base relations. The translation is done so as to provide a problem reduction tree for the next stage of processing. The problem reduction tree is then passed to a processor, which determines a strategy of solution in terms of elementary operations such as "join," "projection," "cross-product," "difference," and so on.

Baldwin, J. F. 1983. A fuzzy relational inference language for expert systems. *Report EM/FS*.

Baldwin describes an implementation on the Honeywell computer at Bristol University, written in MAC-LISP. Some FRIL commands modify the knowledge base, control flow of computation, and send messages through different channels. FRIL also has pointers for self-iteration and for treating relation names as variables. Additional capacities of FRIL include truth functional modification for treating the concatenation of linguistic qualifiers with a relation, inverse truth functional modification for testing the truth of a logical proposition, editing facilities, and display facilities.

Baldwin, J. F. 1983. A knowledge engineering fuzzy inference language—FRIL. *Report EM/FS*.

This work describes facilities to represent probabilistic uncertainties. FRIL is compiled, interpretative, interactive, and more in the style of FORTH than other programming languages. Compilation into an internal code takes place whenever the user adds a new knowledge definition to the knowledge base. Compilation is executed whenever the deduction process, during the answering of a query, requires a use of this definition. FRIL has both a specification and procedural character.

Negoita, C. V., and Ralescu, D. A. 1974. Fuzzy systems and artificial intelligence. *Kybernetes* 3:173–78.

The fuzzy system approach to knowledge tree reduction moves the problem from its initial state, through intermediate states, to the goal state. Thus, a state is a conceptual construct for thinking about and representing knowledge. Given that states have been identified in a conceptual sense, they must be operationalized via some descriptive technique. Operational descriptions that can be used to represent states are vectors, matrices, and predicates. The idea of the knowledge diagram is developed further in Negoita, below.

Negoita, C. V. 1979. On fuzzy systems. In *Advances in fuzzy set theory and applications*, eds. M. Gupta, R. Ragade, and R. Yager. Amsterdam: North-Holland.

The knowledge system must contain information on how states can be altered and under what conditions they can be altered. States are altered by operators. We must specify, therefore, the states to which each operator can be applied and the effect of applying it. This operator is a conceptual construct for thinking about and discussing our knowledge of some application world. Once an operator has been conceptually identified, it must be operationalized via some descriptive technique. That is, knowledge about an operator must be expressed in terms that are comprehensible to any knowledge system. Operationally, there are numerous ways to describe operator knowledge. The operational description method chosen must be compatible with the method selected to represent states. For instance, if states are described as fuzzy objects, then preconditions for the application of the operator should be described as fuzzy objects as well. The concept of *pullback* as a limit diagram in the category of fuzzy objects can represent a family of operators, and in this way a theory of knowledge trees can be developed.

The next two papers describe work done at the laboratory Langages et Systèmes Informatiques at the University Paul Sabatier, Toulouse, France.

Prade, H. 1983. Approximate and plausible reasoning: the state of the art. Paper presented at the IFAC Symposium on Fuzzy Information, Knowledge Representation, and Decision Analysis, July 1983, Marseilles, France.

This paper is a synthesis of different mathematical approaches to uncertainty, including Shafer's belief theory, Zadeh's possibility theory, and probability theory. Approximate reasoning refers to deductive inferences from imprecise premises. These inferences are considered valid in the sense that they extend usual *modus ponens* or *modus tollens* within the framework of axiomatized theories of uncertainty. Plausible reasoning refers to patterns of reasoning that yield uncertain conclusions even when premises are certain.

Martin-Clouaire, R., and Prade, H. 1983. On the problem of representation and propagation of uncertainty. Paper presented at the 2d Annual Conference of the North American Fuzzy Information Processing (NAFIP), June 1983, at Schenectady, New York.

The problems of matching and propagating deductive inference and combination mechanisms are considered in the context of imprecision.

CHAPTER SIX

Knowledge Engineering in Decision Support Systems

An expert system, as its name implies, is an information system that gives the user the ability to pose and obtain answers to questions relating to the information stored in a knowledge base. Typically, such systems possess a nontrivial inferential capability and, in particular, have the capability to infer from premises that are imprecise, vague, or open-textured.

The success of such a system depends on a knowledge engineer's ability to extract information from a human expert and translate it into representations from which the system can make user-invisible inferences.

There are numerous existing systems in use, particularly in the field of medical diagnosis, based either on symbolic manipulation or on approximate reasoning, but management support systems give the best evidence of the potential of these techniques.

JUDGMENT AND INFORMATION IN DECISION MAKING

Let us begin by asking how a manager needing to make a decision handles an information system. The inputs necessary to make a decision come from two sources. One is what we call human judgment. It is the experience, the expertise, the feelings, and the knowledge that constitute judgment. The second is what we call information—a processed set of data that a person needs to reach a decision.

Let us now look at the spectrum of decision types. At one end of the spectrum there is the unstructured decision—a decision in which the key ingredient is judgment. Very little input or information affects the judgment. As a simple example, the judges picking Miss America make a purely unstructured decision. They rely on their judgment alone.

At the other end of the spectrum is the structured decision. That is, if a given a set of data and a precise algorithm to massage the data exist, a decision can be reached. In these cases, the business decision maker has been replaced by a computer. Given a certain amount of information and a certain algorithm, one can make a decision. There are many examples. Linear programming techniques can run an on-line refinery to produce the desired preset results. In effect, these are structured decisions for which a human being is no longer needed in an operational sense.

The development of techniques for this kind of automated decision making (for example, payroll generation, oil refinery operation, and inventory control systems) was the initial goal of early data processing. This style of decision making got the semistructured decision maker— the guy in the middle who needs both information and judgment— into trouble.

To understand why, consider the development of a typical MIS system in the 1970s. In a typical situation, a systems analyst from data processing would try to find out which reports might be automated. From these reports, the analyst would generate a data base and a process that could deliver those same reports. The reports might even be delivered on-line. The first time a decision maker used those reports, the decision maker would ask, "Can we look at the data differently?" Now, the systems analyst may have spent two or three years developing this system, but almost immediately it failed to meet the needs of the decision maker because the system could not vary the output.

A decision system based on the fuzzy set approach is a good example of a system evolving into a decision support system. In essence, the job of a decision support system is to move a decision maker, wherever he or she is along the spectrum of structured and unstructured, toward structured decision making. In other words, its job is to make decision making easier and more structured—to provide information that makes decision making more orderly. Fuzzy set technology takes into account professional expertise and judgments.

The broad outlines of the discipline of computerized decision support have begun to take shape only recently. The term *decision support* first began appearing in the titles of conferences and research papers in the early 1970s. Decision support appears to be an outgrowth of management information systems (MIS), which in turn stem from data base management, which has its roots in information retrieval (Negoita, 1970). There is no clear delimitation between any two adjacent areas in this fourfold progression. However, the progression reflects a broadening of scope and a shifting of emphasis.

As a discipline, decision support includes the other three areas. It differs from the discipline of management information systems in its emphasis on incorporating models into the information system software. This issue certainly was not ignored in the MIS area, but neither was it emphasized. Decision support systems may be considered a renaming of MIS. The new name, IMS (intelligent management systems) calls attention to the emphasis on artificial intelligence approaches and the potential for their incorporation into computer system software. Artificial intelligence emphasizes natural language processing. Because fuzziness is a property of natural language, fuzzy set technology seems useful for understanding and expressing the problems an MIS designer faces.

Planning systems deal with the future. By definition, therefore, data values are unknown and uncertain, and have to be estimated. The purpose of planning is to project how the corporation would perform under unexpected circumstances. For this reason, any planning system must be able to handle both logic and data flexibility. Single-value data forecasts leading to projections of company performance are of limited value; the user, working interactively with the system, needs to explore a whole range of possible futures.

Within planning systems, one has to distinguish between (1) purely financial representations of a corporation and its performance and (2) a fully "corporate model," which in general encompasses nonfinancial aspects of corporate operation, such as capacity, material procurement, marketing, and other aspects critical to the organization's performance. All these aspects are subject to uncertainty.

When management science began to promote mathematical modeling and simulation as aids in planning, it was hoped that computers and computer-based tools would address planning problems directly. Hopes for closer management involvement in the development of management information systems are unwarranted because of two major defects of many existing systems. First is the problem of speed. New systems cannot be set up, and old ones cannot be modified, fast enough to keep up with the constantly changing needs of management. Second, managers cannot apply the model without the aid of specialists. Because of the difficulty of communicating with the technical staff, managers and their support groups are often isolated from their problem-solving tools.

Executives, planning analysts, and intermediaries need direct access to computer-based tools in a kind of personal dialogue. A major shift in this direction began in about 1975 when fuzzy set technology appeared. The possibility of an interactive relationship between the decision maker and the computer appeared feasible because the concept of fuzzy set allows for the explicit consideration of the irreplaceable commodity called "professional expertise and judgment." The development of new planning systems able to work with fuzzy parameters offers users a superb gain in human effectiveness.

Over the last decade, management science has recognized the importance of the systems approach—of the fact that the interaction between the components of a system is often more important than the separate components themselves. Production, financing, economics, and human personnel are not separate but related subjects.

Another challenge to management is the realm of long-range planning. Because time and changes over time are central to the manager's task, a useful planning model must be dynamic. Dynamic models have proved indispensable in designing planning models when corporate management must cope with transient growth, business fluctuation, and uncertainty. In recent years, it has become possible to formulate realistic dynamic models of industrial behavior. Both objective and subjective factors can be included in such a formulation.

Model-building technique and computational cost no longer limit the system under study. Systems theory improves our understanding of how parts interact over time. In the formulation of dynamic models, no distinction is made between corporations and complete economies. No arbitrary distinctions can be drawn between microeconomics and macroeconomics. The same approaches are taken; the same principles apply.

Many discount the potential utility of dynamic models on the assumption that data are usually inadequate. This position reflects the general misunderstanding that a mathematical model cannot be used until every parameter is known to a highly accurate degree. This misconception often leads to the omission of admittedly highly significant subjective evaluations. To omit professional expertise and judgment is equivalent to saying they have no effect. The fuzzy set approach reflects a different attitude toward data and their accuracy. Vagueness need not be eliminated in models if we can use a mechanism to model vagueness. The following pages explore such a mechanism in detail.

QUALITATIVE INQUIRIES

To understand the potential power of approximate reasoning, consider a data base inquiry (Wynne, 1982). Suppose you have a data base of firms that are candidates for acquisition. You wish to find the subset of such candidates that are of attractive size and profitability. Using a conventional or quantitative search criterion set, you might search for firms with sales equal to or greater than $1000 and with a profit margin equal to or greater than 14 percent. With approximate reasoning you could, alternatively, phrase your request as "Find those firms with high sales and acceptable margins." Membership in the fuzzy set "high sales" is defined as 0 below 600 and 1 above 1150. Membership in the fuzzy set "acceptable margins" is defined as 0 below 12 percent and 1 above 18 percent.

The table below shows an 11-firm sample portion of the data base. The quantitative and the qualitative inquiry responses are also shown.

| | | | Responses | |
Firm	Sales	Margin %	Quantity	Quality
A	500	7	0	0
B	600	14	0	0
C	800	17	0	0.52
D	850	12	0	0
E	900	18	0	0.80
F	1000	15	1	0.36
G	1100	14	1	0.19
H	1200	13	0	0.10
I	1300	13	0	0.10
J	1400	6	0	0
K	1500	12	0	0

The quantitative inquiry response identifies two firms, F and G. All others are too small and/or not profitable enough, and thus are passed over. By contrast, the qualitative inquiry returns six candidate firms. However, the key difference is that the qualitative inquiry finds two new firms, E and C, that meet the user's needs more fully than firms F and G do. In addition, the qualitative inquiry returns firms H and I, saying, in essence, "Here are two firms that meet your size criteria but are weak in profitability." By any standard, the qualitative inquiry is more productive in finding candidate firms as the *user* would perceive candidate firms. Firms E and C were cited because "these firms are almost big enough and are very profitable."

This example is typical of REVEAL, a new decision support system developed by Decision Products, Inc. REVEAL provides a true, general-purpose corporate modeling system based on approximate reasoning

(Jones and Morton, 1982). Two ideas led Decision Products to introduce linguistic variables in database retrieval—the rejection of the opinion that human reasoning can be specified and refined to fit exact formal logic, and the assumption that the power of human reasoning lies, by contrast, in its ability to handle inexact concepts. The model's linguistic variable represents the fundamentally imprecise human perception of physical reality, as embodied in such qualifying words as *good, profitable,* and so on.

Inquiries of the data base may be expressed in essentially standard retrieval language if the data base contains summary details on a range of companies. A classical data retrieval specification returns a sharply defined set from the data base.

Suppose the user asks the data base to retrieve a set of companies for the purpose of evaluating candidates for acquisition or building a qualified prospect list. The standard deterministic rules of computer language insist that we employ arbitrary cutoff points. These cutoffs may not reflect the purpose or intent of the user adequately. That user hardly means that at sales of 999 the candidate corporation is of no interest whatsoever, whereas at sales of 1001 it is suddenly as interesting as it possibly can be. More likely, the user means that he or she starts to become interested in a company when its sales approach that value. Only the limitation of the retrieval language forces the user into spurious precision.

With REVEAL one can rephrase this data base inquiry to take advantage of linguistic variables. Linguistic variables permit the users to express themselves more nearly in natural language and also generate additional information concerning the data retrieved.

A key to this and other applications of approximate reasoning is that user specification of the degree of membership function is soundly based on research. This research shows that the approximate reasoning calculus produces implied set membership measures that are replicable across people and conform to independent user appraisal. Approximate reasoning appears to be a valid way to externalize peoples' perceptions of linguistic (qualitative) variables and their interactions.

Management science deals with complex systems that can be described in many ways. A basic question is how different descriptions of the same system relate to one another. To investigate this question, we regard a description as a mapping defined on the space of alternatives. Different descriptions place different evaluations on the set of alternatives and, in particular, provide different orders. The goal is to group individual orders into larger synthesis. The mathematical theory of fuzzy system explains why this *pullback* in the structure of evaluations is possible.

NUMERIC DATA BASES AND LINGUISTIC QUERIES

To see how approximate reasoning adds the concept of linguistic variable to the facilities at the user's disposal in structuring retrieval queries across a data base, we need to explore the mechanism of qualitative inquiry further.

Assume the following data base (Jones, 1983):

Company	Employees	Sales	Gross profit
A	3	200	40
B	10	1100	110
C	11	1000	160
D	9	800	120
E	8	500	55
F	14	1200	115
G	12	1300	200
H	2	100	20
I	6	400	10

If we specify SALES GREATER THAN 1000 the system will retrieve the following data:

Company	Employees	Sales	Gross profit
B	10	1100	110
F	14	1200	115
G	12	1300	200

Now suppose we specify the retrieval query with a linguistic descriptor: SALES ARE HIGH.

Unless the descriptor HIGH is in its memory, the computer will not be able to make the retrieval. In other words, before we use a linguistic value, the value has to be specified in a vocabulary. To specify means to give a table describing the fuzzy subset HIGH defined on the set of SALES, as in the following table:

HIGH	
SALES	Truth Value
0	0
750	0
900	0.08
1050	0.32
1200	0.68
1350	0.92
1500	1

If this table is used, the column SALES in the original data base receives degrees of membership. In answer to the query specification SALES ARE HIGH, the system yields the following:

		Answer		
Company	Employees	Sales	Gross profits	Degree
B	10	1100	110	0.39
C	11	1000	160	0.18
D	9	800	120	0.01
F	14	1200	115	0.68
G	12	1300	200	0.82

There is no limit to the complexity of the predicate. We can distinguish among companies according to BEAUTIFUL SALES, SPLENDID PROFITS, or SMALL NUMBER OF EMPLOYEES if clear definitions of these terms exist in the vocabulary. The predicates can contain many clauses, linked by the operators AND or OR.

The degree of membership can define a new object—a fuzzy relation—which can be labeled and stored in the vocabulary. For instance, the previous answer can be labeled

COMPANIES WITH HIGH SALES

and stored under that name. Different projections of this fuzzy relation can be labeled separately.

Although many problems can be solved by keying in the appropriate numbers and symbols, the greatest benefits of programming the decision support system in APL become evident when we use named functions and data. Because a single name may refer to a large array of data, we can simply key in the name rather than all of its members. If one may choose a computer language in which to implement a semantic system, there is no doubt that APL should be the choice. APL syntax was designed to be similar to that of natural language, an elegant feature those implementing approximate reasoning techniques in decision support systems can exploit. If we define fuzzy subsets as arrays, hedges (such as *very*) as monadic functions, and all other categories as dyadic functions, statements in natural language will also be correct APL statements assigning meaning to words.

Once a function has been defined or data have been collected under a name, it is usually desirable to retain the significance of the names for the vocabulary. For this reason, APL systems are organized around the concept of a workspace, which might be thought of as a notebook in which all the different items needed for approximate reasoning are recorded.

To start, the stored workspace containing the vocabulary package is activated by a simple system command

)LOAD

The response indicates when the vocabulary was last saved. To learn the content of the vocabulary, we can list the names of variables and defined functions from the beginning. The system command

)VARS

an abbreviation of variables, produces an alphabetic listing of stored variables.

As users, we want to find out what functions—hedges or operators—are in the vocabulary. The system command

)FNS

which works exactly as)VARS does, lists the functions.

Suppose a decision support system accepts approximate reasoning techniques and therefore linguistic retrieval specifications. If the system is programmed in APL, the user can inspect the vocabulary if it is installed. The user will see that synonyms for the operators and conjunctions are available, allowing statements to be written in natural language. For instance, valid synonyms for IS and AND appear in the table below.

IS	AND
ARE	BUT
SHOULD BE	WHILE
WOULD BE	WHILST
MIGHT BE	THOUGH
MAY BE	ALTHOUGH
COULD BE	WHEN
OUGHT TO BE	
MUST BE	

The user will also see a default set of "noise" words, such as

MY YOUR OUR THEIR   A AN THE
HIS HER ITS   THIS THAT THESE THOSE

Noise words contribute nothing to the logical values of the assertions but make the statements more like natural English.

First of all, the user will find *primary terms*, such as

HIGH, LOW, MEDIUM, ACCEPTABLE, UNKNOWN

hedges, such as

ABOVE, BELOW, AROUND, LOWER, RATHER, MORE OR LESS
VERY, NOT, NEITHER, POSSIBLY, INDEED

connectives, such as

AND, OR, PLUS, MINUS, EXCEPT

and *system variables*, such as

COMPANIES WITH HIGH SALES

It is almost certain that the user will never be satisfied with the vocabulary. Users always need more. For instance, the table

COMPANIES WITH ACCEPTABLE PROFITS/SALES

may be necessary. ACCEPTABLE is a fuzzy subset defined in the vocabulary, but the report PROFITS/SALES must be defined. The symbol / must be replaced with the symbol ÷ for division in APL. WITH is a pointer defined in the beginning vocabulary. A retrieval specification, such as

COMPANIES WITH ACCEPTABLE PROFITS ÷ SALES

or equivalently

COMPANIES WITH ACCEPTABLE PROFITS DIVIDED BY SALES

will produce an answer such as

Company	Sales	Profits	Degree
C	1000	160	1
D	800	120	0.69
G	1300	200	0.93

where the membership degree arises from the fuzzy subset ACCEPTABLE.

POLICY ROUTINES

Because they are based in radically different programming styles, knowledge systems differ from traditional computer programs in a variety of ways. Knowledge systems differ most visibly from standard computer systems in their capability to *interact* intelligently with their users.

Quantitative analysis has proved an indispensable tool in business because of its deductive power. A quantitative model is *deductive* if there are consistent rules for deriving the output values from known input values. Output is achieved automatically when the variables are numeric (their values are numbers) and when their interrelations are expressed by mathematical formulas. Dynamic models, when used for a strictly mathematical analysis of causes and effects, are common tools for forecasting and planning because the computer can do much of the heavy work of model construction and analysis.

Imagine that the user is interested in setting a price for a low-valued product, for instance, a packaged food item, and is working in an elementary crisp context. To set the price, the user can consider DIRECT COST and VOLUME as input variables and SALES MARGIN, GROSS SALES, and GROSS PROFIT as state variables in a dynamic model whose equations are as follows:

$$\text{SALES MARGIN} \leftarrow \text{PRICE} - \text{DIRECT COST}$$
$$\text{GROSS SALES} \leftarrow \text{VOLUME} \times \text{PRICE}$$
$$\text{GROSS PROFIT} \leftarrow \text{SALES MARGIN} \times \text{VOLUME}$$

If the DIRECT COST is compounded monthly for 3 months at 16 percent for a VOLUME of 100 and a PRICE of 7, the trajectory describing the evolution of the state variables will be

	Jan	Feb	Mar	Apr	May	Jun
VOLUME	100	100	100	100	100	100
PRICE	7	7	7	7	7	7
DIRECT COST	3	3.04	3.08	3.13	3.17	3.21
SALES MARGIN	4	3.96	3.92	3.87	3.83	3.79
GROSS SALES	700	700	700	700	700	700
GROSS PROFIT	400	396	392	387	383	379

Instead of treating the PRICE as a purely numeric input, the user can build a *policy routine* and treat PRICE as a *linguistic variable*. The first thing to do is to build a vocabulary and create some qualifiers describing the user's perception of the pricing problem. If that perception is

PRICE SHOULD BE LOW
PRICE SHOULD BE ABOUT DOUBLE THE DIRECT COST

the user must define LOW and ABOUT in the vocabulary. To define meaning is to specify tables.

LOW		ABOUT 6	
5	1	5	0.5
5.5	0.92	5.5	0.7
6	0.88	6	1.0
6.5	0.72	6.5	0.7
7	0.5	7	0.5
7.5	0.28	7.5	0.2
8	0.13	8	0
8.5	0.03	8.5	0
9	0	9	0
10	0	10	0

ABOUT approximates the value of the argument. This hedge creates a fuzzy subset centered around a scalar value. If the argument is already fuzzy, the hedge broadens the spread of the fuzzy subset. In that case, the numeric value of PRICE will represent that value in the intersection of the two fuzzy propositions having the maximal degree of membership. In other words

$$\text{max min } (f_{\text{LOW}}, f_{\text{ABOUT 2} \times \text{DIRECT COST}})$$

Because DIRECT COST evolves over time, the maximum of the intersection shifts, and the trajectory will be

	Jan	Feb	Mar	Apr	May	Jun
VOLUME	100	100	100	100	100	100
PRICE	5.6	5.7	5.75	5.8	5.85	5.95
DIRECT COST	3	3.04	3.08	3.13	3.17	3.21
SALES MARGIN	2.60	2.66	2.67	2.67	2.68	2.74
GROSS SALES	560	570	575	580	585	595
GROSS PROFIT	260	266	267	267	268	274

Suppose the user's perception of the pricing problem changes, and the user wants to add another policy routine, for instance, a routine that takes competitive activity into account. The user can then introduce another fuzzy subset resulting from the fuzzy proposition

PRICE SHOULD BE NEAR THE OPPOSITION

The new fuzzy subset can be added to and intersected with the others.

PLANNING AND FORECASTING WITH DYNAMIC ROBUST MODELS

A dynamic model is essentially a set of equations whose variables can be divided into input variables (or exogenous variables) and state variables (or endogenous variables). Dynamic models can be used to combine, in a strictly mathematical manner, an analysis of causes and effects, with or without time lags and various feedback relationships.

The abstract definition of a dynamic model has grown out of various applications in control theory. But dynamic models have been

used to model processes in other areas also. Above all, many macro-
economic models are dynamic, but applications in microeconomics
also exist (Negoita, 1979).

A main reason why dynamic models are so frequently used as
forecasting and planning tools is that computers can do much of the
heavy work of model construction and model analysis. The computer
can be used to estimate equation parameters, to analyze the dynamic
properties of the model, to forecast, and to plan with the aid of the
model. A number of user-directed programs and even programming
languages have been especially constructed for simulating and analyzing dynamic models.

A fundamental postulate is that the system or process to be modeled can be described by a set of state variables that are functions of
time. The state of a system at time k is identified with the set of values
$x_1(k), x_2(k), \ldots, x_n(k)$. The set of all possible states of a dynamic model
is called the *state space*.

Normally, a system can be controlled by external factors. The control can be characterized by a set of input variables, also functions of
time, denoted $u_1(k), u_2(k), \ldots, u_m(k)$. The set of all possible input vectors
is called the *input space*. Any change in the state can be defined as a
function of the previous state $x(k)$, the present state $x(k+1)$, the previous input $u(k)$, and the time k.

$$x(k+1) = F[x(k), u(k), k]$$

This rather abstract definition of the discrete deterministic dynamic
model is best illustrated by example. Consider a production system
modeled in terms of the actual production, x_1; the desired production,
x_3; the inventory, x_2; the delivery, d; and the investment, u.

The state representation could be

$$x_1(k+1) = x_1(k) + [x_3(k) - x_1(k)]$$
$$x_2(k+1) = x_2(k) + x_1(k) - d(k)$$
$$x_3(k+1) = x_3(k) + u(k)$$

The state equation describes a flow at various moments and shows the
connections between the indicators chosen to describe a production
system. These connections reflect an existing pattern of organization.

Although a variable may be classified as an input variable in a
dynamic model, it is not always possible for humans to control the
values of the variable, or sometimes the control may be very restricted.
Such is the case of delivery, d.

A simulation of a dynamic model during a time interval, T, consists
of supplying initial values for both the state variables and the input
variables during T and then using the model equations to compute the

values of the state variables for a number of times during T. With a computer, the simulations can be programmed and performed rapidly.

A main advantage of using dynamic models is that they are suitable for policy experiments. If we assume that reliable forecasts for the external variables are available, then by studying the behavior of the model for various future values of the policy variables, we may get a rough idea of which plans lead to the most desirable combinations of values for the input and state variables. Necessary prerequisites for this method of planning are (1) some knowledge of the dynamic properties of the model and (2) enough energy to investigate a large number of future policy variable values in a systematic manner.

By repeated simulations trials and by learning from mistakes, we can select those future plans that have acceptable consequences.

Trial-and-error with a dynamic model is not an efficient method of finding the optimal plan for the future; also, with this method there is no guarantee that the optimal plan will ever be found. For this reason, we may try to use certain results from control theory to construct the optimal planning problem as a mathematical optimization problem. Such an optimization problem has five components:

1. A dynamic model
2. A time interval for which the optimal planning is to be computed
3. A set of initial values of the state variables, and, possibly, a set of final values that the final state variables must reach
4. Restrictions on the state variables and input variables
5. A function to measure the utility of the behavior of the model that measures the planner's goals

When these five components are given, the optimization problem becomes finding which control variable values during the time interval maximize the utility of the behavior of the model.

In certain special cases, general algorithms for solving this optimization problem exist. The cases most extensively studied are linear time-invariant models.

Dynamic models are, no doubt, among the best tools for forecasting and planning. The conceptual framework is rich enough to cover most mathematically formulated models in which temporal aspects are central, and it allows precise formulations of causal relationships and mutual dependencies between variables. The equations in a model are formal representations of the structure of a complex situation. Our intuitions and theoretical education may be of good use when we formulate the equations. But when the pieces of the model are assembled, we need precise data from the decision maker.

The use of a model is affected by many characteristics of the domain, such as the size of the solution space and errors in the data.

These are the requirements for task simplicity:

1. The data and model should be reliable.

2. The data and model should be static.

3. The space of possible solutions should be small.

On the surface, these requirements may seem quite mild. Indeed, there is a widely held belief among people who have not looked closely into planning that most problems satisfy these requirements. On closer examination, however, most real situations fail to meet these requirements.

The first requirement is that the data be reliable in real applications. Few sources of data meet this requirement. The second requirement is intended to avoid the problem of reasoning with time-dependent data. In real applications this is almost impossible.

A common issue in the analysis of large-scale systems is the appropriate reduction of dimension so that the output of the resulting system displays, to a certain extent, the most important features of the output of the original system. In general, one tries to aggregate current variables into a few manageable indices that are sufficient for decision making. This is the case, for instance, for economic models, which usually call for reducing a large and detailed model to a simple one that displays the variables important to decision-making policy.

Consider a state equation that describes production flow at various moments and shows how much should be invested at specific moments to ensure that production quotas imposed by strategic planning are met.

$$x_1(k+1) = x_1(k) + \alpha[x_2(k) - x_1(k)] - d(k)$$
$$x_2(k+1) = x_2(x) + u(k)$$

where x_1 means stock, x_2 means capacity, u means new capacity, and d means delivery. The underlying philosophy of the model is the following: the stock of today equals the stock of yesterday plus the amount produced between yesterday and today.

Often the coefficient α has to be thought of as a fuzzy set

$$\alpha : R \rightarrow [0,1]$$

that can be given as a rule by an expert, that is, an individual with considerable knowledge and understanding of a particular field. The assessment of the parameter can be organized to show quantitatively the relative merits of alternatives suggested by assessors. Working with fuzzy tolerances instead of numbers seems to be exactly the way people cope with their environment.

The ability to work with models having fuzzy parameters means robustness, and to permit this formulation we must define some operations with fuzzy sets. For instance, if we work with a linear model then we can add two fuzzy sets and multiply a fuzzy set by a number. Consider two fuzzy sets

$$f_1: R \rightarrow [0,1]$$
$$f_2: R \rightarrow [0,1]$$

Their sum can be defined as

$$(f_1 + f_2)(z) = \sup_{w_1 + w_2 = z} \min (f_1(w_1), f_2(w_2))$$

The fuzzy version of the model can be written as

$$x_1(k+1) - (1 - \underset{\sim}{\alpha}) x_1(k) - \underset{\sim}{\alpha} x_2(k) \subseteq \underset{\sim}{d}(k)$$

where $\sim$ means fuzzy set. Having brought matters to this point, we are ready to pass to the difficult matter of defuzzification. First, we make the important observation that, according to a representation theorem (Negoita and Ralescu, 1975), any fuzzy set may be represented by a family of sets, called level sets. A level set of a fuzzy set is a crisp set

$$A_n^i = \{r \in R / f_i(r) > n, n \in [0,1]\}$$

with the evident properties

$$n_1 \leq n_2 \rightarrow A_{n_2}^i \subset A_{n_1}^i$$
$$f_i(r) < f_j(r) \rightarrow A_n^i \subset A_n^j$$

We are now able to replace the fuzzy version of the state equation with a number of level equations. For instance, if we consider three levels then the state equation becomes

$$x_1(k+1) - (1 - [\alpha_m, \alpha_M]) x_1(k) - [\alpha_m, \alpha_M] x_2(k) \subset [d_m, d_M]$$
$$x_1(k+1) - (1 - [\alpha'_m, \alpha'_M]) x_1(k) - [\alpha'_m, \alpha'_M] x_2(k) \subset [d'_m, d'_M]$$
$$x_1(k+1) - (1 - [\alpha''_m, \alpha''_M]) x_1(k) - [\alpha''_m, \alpha''_M] x_2(k) \subset [d''_m, d''_M]$$

Further, we can convert the equation involving inclusion into one involving inequalities (Negoita, 1981).

For instance, the first line becomes

$$x_1(k+1) - (1 - \alpha_M) x_1(k) - \alpha_M x_2(k) < d_M$$
$$x_1(k+1) - (1 - \alpha_m) x_1(k) - \alpha_m x_2(k) > d_m$$

Incorporating imprecision, and thus flexibility, enlarges the problem dimension. An important advantage of this method is that decision makers are no longer compelled to state parameters exactly. Exact statements, by contrast, are absolutely necessary with conventional techniques. Admitting imprecision in problem formulation might help greatly in situations where boundaries are not sharp; also, incorporating imprecise constraints makes the techniques flexible. The second great advantage of this method is that the fuzzy model can be converted into a conventional model and can therefore be solved by conventional techniques. This last fact is obviously important because of the relatively large number of existing techniques and algorithms.

In other words, fuzzy set theory has extended traditional models so that they can cope with vagueness, or, stated another way, the traditional models have been extended to cope with a broader part of reality.

PULLBACK IN FLEXIBLE PROGRAMMING

Often, decision support systems have to solve problems of minimizing or maximizing a linear function in the presence of linear constraints of inequality and/or equality. For example, consider the following capital budgeting problem.

A construction project has funding requirements over the next 4 years of $2 million, $4 million, $8 million, and $5 million, respectively. Assume that all of the money for a given year is required at the beginning of the year and that a city intends to sell enough long-term bonds to cover the project funding requirements. All of these bonds, regardless of when they are sold, mature on the same date in a distant future year. The long-term bond market interest rates for the next 4 years are projected to be 7 percent, 6 percent, 6.5 percent, and 7.5 percent, respectively. Bond interest paid will commence 1 year after the project is completed and will continue for 20 years, after which the bonds will be paid off. During the same period, the city can earn short-term interest on time deposits. The short-term rates are projected to be 6 percent, 5.5 percent, and 4.5 percent, respectively, because the city will clearly not invest money in short-term deposits during the fourth year.

The problem is to find the city's optimal strategy for selling bonds and depositing funds in time accounts in order to complete the construction project. A linear programming model can give the answer to this problem

Minimize $20(0.07)x_1 - 20(0.06)x_2 - 20(0.065)x_3 - 20(0.075)x_4$

$$
\begin{aligned}
\text{Subject to } x_1 - y_1 &= 2 \\
1.06y_1 - x_2 - y_2 &= 4 \\
1.055y_2 - x_3 - y_3 &= 8 \\
1.045y_3 - x_4 &= 5
\end{aligned}
$$

where x_j is the amount of bonds sold at the beginning of year j and y_i is the money placed in time deposits at the beginning of year i. The problem can be stated more conveniently in matrix notation

$$\text{Minimize} \quad cx$$
$$\text{Subject to} \quad Ax = b$$

where c is a row vector, x and b are column vectors, and A is a matrix. The set of all feasible vectors x constitutes the feasible space, and the linear programming problem is to find a feasible vector that minimizes the objective function cx.

Now, instead of treating the funding requirements as pure numeric input, the decision maker can build policy routines; that is, treat funding requirements as linguistic propositions such as "close to $2 million" or "acceptable." The first thing to do is to build a vocabulary and create some qualifiers describing the decision maker's perception of the funding problem. These are fuzzy sets, and each constraint may be written as a composition.

$$A_k \qquad \text{fuzzy set}$$
$$\text{feasible vector} \to \text{numbers} \to \text{unit interval}$$

A fuzzy linear programming problem can give the answer to the new problem.

If we denote by x_5 a new variable

$$x_5 = \min F_i(x)$$
$$F_i(x) = (B_i - \sum_{j=1}^{4} a_{ij} x_j) / (B_i - b_i)$$
$$F_{\text{CLOSE TO } b} : [b,B] \to [0,1]$$

$[b,B]$ is the interval where b can take values, then the fuzzy linear programming problem becomes

$$\text{Maximize} \quad x_5$$
$$\text{Subject to} \quad \sum_{j=1}^{4} a_{ij} x_j - (B_i - b_i) x_5 \leqslant B_i$$

No matter how we define the fuzzy set describing the perception of the decision maker, the decision support system can make explicit the subjective nature of any choice made on the basis of fuzzy information. The effect of a policy routine is pulled back along the linear function described by the matrix A according to the diagram

$$A_k^{-1} \text{ (policy routine)} \longrightarrow \text{policy routine}$$
$$\downarrow \qquad\qquad\qquad\qquad\qquad \downarrow$$
$$\text{feasible vector} \xrightarrow{\quad A_k \quad} \text{numbers}$$

SUMMARY

1. A decision support system can be defined as an interactive computer system that directly assists executives in decision-making tasks. Because of the computer's vast memory resources and its information processing speed, decision support systems have the potential to be part of an effective man-machine problem-solving system.

2. Decision support systems are most appropriate for semistructured problems, that is, for problems with sufficient structure for computer and analytic aids to be of value but problems for which human judgment is still essential.

3. Decision support systems support but do not replace managerial judgment.

4. The primary concern of this book is with problems of creating knowledge-based decision support systems that permit policy routine formulation in natural language.

5. In particular, this book examines two separate but related aspects of fuzzy linear programming: flexible and robust programming.

6. Flexible programming is linear programming with fuzzy feasible spaces specified by fuzzy constraints.

7. Robust programming is linear programming with fuzzy numbers as coefficients.

8. Both flexible and robust programming problems can have precise solutions. Intelligent decision support systems must help us take precise actions in the face of imprecise information. Using fuzzy set theory, we can build algorithms to meet this task.

9. In the case of robust programming, these algorithms are based on the theorem of representation, which allows any fuzzy subset to be represented by a family of crisp level sets.

10. These algorithms can be used to generate production rules for programs that solve problems too difficult to be solved by humans alone.

READINGS

Jones, P. L., and Morton, W. E. 1982. REVEAL. In *Computer based planning systems*, eds. T. Naylor and M. Mann. Oxford, Ohio: Planning Executive Institute.

The authors describe a commercially available software product that represents a breakthrough in policy modeling. REVEAL is a significant step forward in providing, through the use of approximate reasoning, a facility for capturing and manipulating judgmental and attitudinal information. Most importantly, REVEAL is not a standalone, laboratory, or experimental tool. It is a fully integrated part of a complete decision support and modeling system. REVEAL is a decision support system generator that enables users to extend conventional quantitative modeling analysis. The user describes contingent policies in natural language as an integral part of the model. Periodically, quantitative modeling results are interpreted through qualitative policy statements. As a result, quantitative model parameters may be reset to simulate the desired management policy. Thus, the trajectory of the what-if scenario under scrutiny is controlled by the policy presumed to apply. Via approximate reasoning based on fuzzy logic, the user can tailor standard quantitative models to qualitatively expressed judgments.

Decision Products Services, Inc. 1982. *REVEAL system and user guide*. vol 2, *Approximate reasoning*. Mountain View, Calif.: Decision Products Services, Inc., Fairchild Drive.

This manual has tutorial material on the subject of fuzzy sets and approximate reasoning and its implementation within REVEAL. The basic objectives of the approximation modes are to allow the creation of models that represent the user's knowledge and to use this knowledge in conjunction with standard deterministic models built into the foundation system.

Negoita, C. V. 1983. Fuzzy sets in decision support systems. *Human Systems Management* 4:27–33.

This paper explains how traditional operations research techniques such as linear programming can be used in the context of decision support systems accepting judgmental and attitudinal information. Due to the existence of a fuzzy arithmetic, parameters in mathematical models can be fuzzy numbers. More details about such models and how they are used in planning can be found in Negoita, 1983 and 1979, below.

Negoita, C. V. 1983. Planning and forecasting with robust dynamic models. *Kybernetes* 12:299–333.

This article is based on the theory of robust programming presented in detail in Negoita, 1979, below.

Negoita, C. V. 1979. *Management applications of system theory*. Basel, Switzerland and Boston: Birkhäuser Verlag.

This book explains some ideas in modern systems theory and shows how they can be applied to certain problems in decision support systems. Growth is viewed as dynamics; planning, as trajectory estimation; and control, as trajectory maintenance. The basic assumptions are (1) that the future is not to be discovered but must be created, (2) that possibility is an efficient uncertainty concept, and (3) that a global approach is preferable to a local one. The message is that system theory can guide us in deriving far-reaching conclusions from clearly stated premises. Innovation, for instance, is an attribute with a clear—although not precise—meaning. We can intuitively assign low or high values to innovation; but if the values are to be numeric, the attributes must be defined operationally. Even attributes with objective scales are evaluated with linguistic values.

A key point in this book is that fuzziness is not a liability. On the contrary, fuzziness makes for robustness. At high levels of complexity, when the model is vague, the use of fuzzy set technology is a way to cope with vagueness. How? By defuzzifying. One possibility explored in this book is given by the theorem of representation, according to which any fuzzy set is a family of crisp sets. More details about the theory of representation can be found in Ralescu, below.

Ralescu, D. A. 1979. A survey of the representation of fuzzy concepts and its applications. In *Advances in fuzzy set theory and applications*, eds. M. Gupta, R. Ragade, and R. Yager. Amsterdam: North-Holland.

This tutorial not only lays out the basic ideas of fuzzy programming but also discusses its applications. The reader interested in further developments, however, should see the proceedings of the seminar on fuzzy sets held at the Department of Mathematics, University Claude-Bernard, Lyons, France, by Professor Ponasse and his group. For applications of fuzzy sets, see Negoita, 1981, below.

Negoita, C. V. 1981. The current interest in fuzzy optimization. *Fuzzy Sets and Systems* 6:262–69.

A certain interpretation of fuzzy programming is proposed. Flexible and robust programming are reviewed and their definitions explicitly identified. Both involve new ways of depicting reality, and fuzziness is a vehicle for conciseness and economy of expression. The same opinion can be found in Kacprzyk, below.

Kacprzyk, J. 1983. *Multistage decision making under fuzziness*. Köln: Verlag TUV Rheinland.

This extensive survey of sequential decision making in a fuzzy environment uses no sophisticated mathematical formalism and keeps the discussion as constructive and algorithmic as possible. The text includes many models of soft-decision situations. Clearly distinct from more traditional monographs, which typically lead the reader through descriptions of different approaches to theoretical analysis, this work, based on the author's findings, leads to practical applications.

The reasoning is dominated by the control paradigm. Postulating the usefulness of analyzing (in control-systemic terms) any situation in which action is taken to attain some desired outcomes, Kacprzyk deals with time-invariant fuzzy systems with nonfuzzy control.

The book begins with an overview of decision making followed by an introduction to the theory of fuzzy sets and fuzzy systems. It concludes with applications. The five central chapters are each a discourse on multistage decision making in a fuzzy environment (with fixed and specified termination time, with implicitly specified termination time, with fuzzy termination time, or with infinite termination time).

One interesting feature is the introduction of relevant practical applications. An important example is the comparison of different socioeconomic development policies for a rural region suffering from the irreversible effects of the migration of young people to urban regions. The migration is caused mainly by the perception of life quality as poor. To stop economic decay, the perceived quality of life must be considerably improved to increase satisfaction. Because the region does not have sufficient funds, external outlays are necessary. The problem is to determine these outlays and their temporal distribution over some planning horizon so that the development goals are best met. Fuzzy sets emerge as a tool for coupling feelings and perceptions of decision makers with data in numeric decision models.

The book elucidates the range of what we understand about decision making in fuzzy environments and illustrates the advantages of opening the mind and allowing judgment and professional expertise to assume their rightful roles in problem evaluation. The author makes an excellent case against economic determinism by pointing out that perceptions of the environment may be just as important as things more readily measured and systematized. Preoccupation with precision can be as intellectually inhibiting as medieval scholasticism. Sorting out the many ideas presented in this book may open up vistas and inspire a more concentrated search for integrated studies in which judgment and professional expertise are accorded the consideration they merit.

Using no sophisticated mathematical formalism, Kacprzyk provides the reader with a methodology mainly developed at the

Systems Research Institute of the Polish Academy of Sciences in Warsaw. Some topics were recently elaborated and refined while the author was visiting the Machine Intelligence Institute at the Hagan School of Business of Iona College in New Rochelle, New York.

Today, management scientists, political economists, sociologists, and behavior researchers all use systems research when working with quantitatively describable phenomena. They all use computers to enhance human thinking when processing empirical questions or fleshing out theories. Such activity, however, requires a methodology for handling linguistic variables in the frameworks of mathematical models, no matter how complicated or how simple they are. This book is a step toward establishing such a methodology. It describes, illustrates, and presents it in a way that is immediately understandable.

Fuzzy linear programming seems to have started with a 1974 paper by Tanaka, Okuda, and Asai. Zimmermann became a major contributor with his work at the University of Aachen in Germany. The following papers are particularly important in the development of fuzzy linear programming.

Tanaka, H., Okuda, T., and Asai, K. 1974. On fuzzy mathematical programming. *Journal of Cybernetics* 3:37–46.

Zimmermann, H. J. 1978. Fuzzy programming and linear programming with several objective functions. *Fuzzy Sets and Systems* 1:45–55.

Verdegay, J. L. 1982. Fuzzy mathematical programming. In *Fuzzy information and decision processes*, eds. M. Gupta and E. Sanchez. Amsterdam: North-Holland.

Verdegay suggests a new method for providing a fuzzy solution to the original fuzzy problem.

Kabbara, G. 1982. New utilization of fuzzy optimization method. In *Fuzzy information and decision processes*, eds. M. Gupta and E. Sanchez. Amsterdam: North-Holland.

Kabbara presents the fuzzy linear programming problem as a solution for the crisp linear programming problem without a solution.

Negoita, C. V., and Stefanescu, A. 1982. On fuzzy optimization. In *Fuzzy information and decision processes*, eds. M. Gupta and E. Sanchez. Amsterdam: North-Holland.

This paper suggests that optimization can be viewed as a problem of internal logic.

CHAPTER SEVEN

Knowledge Engineering in Management Expert Systems

The major force behind the gradual development of aids to decision making is the nature of the decision-making task itself. Mathematical modeling is often put forward as an attractive possibility for prescribing strategies to make an organization behave in some desired way. Modeling is certainly a powerful tool, but many philosophical difficulties must be overcome before it can be applied with confidence to management problems.

One reason is the fuzzy environment. Whether one likes it or not, managers move in a fuzzy environment; decision makers who act to manipulate the world around them cannot and do not make policy decisions only by reducing tradeoffs to numbers. In reality, managers do not always perceive that world with complete accuracy; even when they do, it may still change.

The notions of enduring fuzziness and using fuzziness are enticing, and they offer exciting new approaches to management information systems. *Enduring fuzziness* is the capacity to tolerate linguistic variables in classical decision methods.

WHICH IS BEST? THE LINGUISTIC APPROACH TO DECISION MAKING

Consider the following investment problem: a man has a moderately large amount of capital which he wants to invest to best advantage. In order to act, he wants to make a judgment on the "best advantage." He has selected five possible investment areas (Tong and Bonissone, 1980):

a_1 The commodities market
a_2 The stock market
a_3 Gold and/or diamonds
a_4 Real estate
a_5 Long-term bonds

Fuzzy reasoning is used even at the outset because there is no absolute measure of the best advantage. The most one can do is offer an opinion about the judgment used to select the investment areas— the alternatives in the best advantage category. Furthermore, such a judgment is based on reference to a decision universe. Specifically, before a judgment is rendered, reference is made to such criteria as:

c_1 The risk of losing the capital sum
c_2 The vulnerability of the capital sum to inflation
c_3 The amount of interest received
c_4 The ability to realize the capital sum

One usually does not make judgments immediately but instead evaluates the situation in light of the given set of criteria and then tries to *synthesize* the knowledge. The man might rate the investment alternatives with respect to the criteria above as in the table on page 143. Note that this synthesis is expressed linguistically rather than numerically.

This is another way to write a string of production rules of the form

IF we consider c_4 THEN a_3 is good.

IF one invests in gold THEN the risk of losing the sum is low.

Here the decision is to select one of the alternatives with the additional constraint that the criteria are not equally important but have linguistic weights as in the following fuzzy propositions:

c_1 IS moderately important
The risk of losing the capital IS moderately important.

Therefore, any line of the table giving the linguistic ratings can be read as a production rule. For instance, the first line is:

IF one invests in the commodity market
THEN (1) the moderately important risk of losing capital is high, plus
     (2) the more or less important vulnerability of the capital sum to inflation is more or less high, plus
     (3) the very important amount of interest received is very high, plus
     (4) the more or less unimportant ability to realize the capital is fair

Alternative	Criterion 1 (moderately important)	Criterion 2 (more or less important)	Criterion 3 (very important)	Criterion 4 (more or less unimportant)
a_1	High	More or less high	Very high	Fair
a_2	Fair	Fair	Fair	More or less good
a_3	Low	Fair to more or less low	Fair	Good
a_4	Low	Very low	More or less high	Bad
a_5	Very low	High	More or less low	Very good

Given this statement of the problem, the investor has to select an alternative. The THEN part of the production rule can be interpreted as a measure of each alternative's ability to meet the decision criteria. Therefore, the investor has to compare the THEN part of the five production rules. These are five fuzzy subsets, easily obtained if we observe that all the linguistic values are fuzzy numbers defined on the closed unit interval.

A fuzzy number may be characterized by a 4-tuple (A, B, a, b) where A,B denotes the interval in which the membership degrees are equal to 1 and a, b denotes the interval in which the membership degrees are equal to 0. Notice that crisp numbers can be represented in this form by $(A, A, 0, 0)$, and that interval numbers may be written as $(A, B, 0, 0)$.

Because fuzzy numbers can be added and multiplied, if we translate the linguistic values in the THEN part of the production rules, a *suitability* fuzzy subset can be calculated for each of the alternatives, using, for instance, the following weighted fuzzy sum:

$$\text{Suitability}_i = \sum_{j=1}^{4} \text{weights}_j \cdot \text{ratings}_{ij}$$

The beauty of the method is that only seven basic shapes are used to represent the range of linguistic values, according to the table on page 145 (Bonissone, 1982). This is an example of how one can work with parametric versions of fuzzy subsets rather than the membership functions themselves. In this case, applying the basic arithmetic operations between fuzzy subsets is a matter of following some simple rules for combining the parameters. For instance, the addition becomes

$$(A, B, a, b) + (M, N, m, n) = (A+M, B+N, a+m, b+n)$$

Because the universe of discourse on which the elements of the suitability fuzzy subsets (numbers) are defined is a linearly ordered set, the "best" alternative is the one defined by a suitability fuzzy subset (number) with a peak that lies to the right of all others.

The word *best* is understood here exactly as in any other optimization problem, no matter how sophisticated in its formulation. In any optimization problem according to a *unique* criterion, finding the best alternative means making the alternatives correspond to elements of the real line and exploiting the order structure of this real line. This is exactly what we have done here. The five alternatives were evaluated by five fuzzy numbers, and the one to the right of all others is the largest.

Interpretation when used with

Fuzzy number	c_1	c_2	c_3	c_4	Weights
(0, 0, 0, 0.2)	Very High	Very High	Very Low	Very Bad	Very unimportant
(0, 0.1, 0, 0.2)	High	High	Low	Bad	Unimportant
(0.2, 0.2, 0.2, 0.2)	More or less high	More or less high	More or less low	More or less bad	More or less unimportant
(0.5, 0.5, 0.2, 0.2)	Fair	Fair	Fair	Fair	Indifferent
(0.8, 0.8, 0.2, 0.2)	More or less low	More or less low	More or less high	More or less good	More or less important
(0.9, 1, 0.2, 0)	Low	Low	High	Good	Important
(1, 1, 0.2, 0)	Very low	Very low	Very high	Very good	Very important

The deep significance of this approach is that we moved the decision problem from a space with many criteria to a space with only one criterion, the only natural criterion—numbers.

We can thus answer a very difficult question, such as

WHICH IS THE BEST?

which requires a lot of intelligence indeed. In this case, the production system is no more than individual IF-THEN production rules interacting with each other by means of a data base.

In knowledge systems using production rules for symbolic manipulation, the only way that one rule is connected to another is if the right-side variables of one rule match the left-side variables of the other. In our example, they are connected by linguistic values. A semantic system increases the power of the production system, and we can streamline the application of fuzzy set theory in a way that lets us manipulate large inventories of knowledge.

WHAT IS COMING?
DECISION SUPPORT WITH ADVISORY SYSTEMS

We are interested in finding automated procedures for extracting information from knowledge bases that contain linguistic representations. One worry is that production systems may break down if the amount of knowledge is too large, for then the number of production rules grows beyond reasonable bounds. Therefore it is reasonable to work with as few rules as possible. Is this possible? Of course it is. See the section in Chapter Five, "Value Questions."

That section shows that an important application of compositional inference is to knowledge of the type

VARIABLE 1 IS A
IF VARIABLE 1 IS B THEN VARIABLE 2 IS C

Using the rule of compositional inference, we can infer a value for VARIABLE 2.

$$f_{\text{VARIABLE 2}}(y) = \max_{x} \quad \min\left(f_{\text{VARIABLE 1}}(x), f_{\text{RULE}}(x, y)\right)$$

Therefore, we can use the same production rule to infer as many values for VARIABLE 2 as values for VARIABLE 1.

The production rules are obtained from human experts, but the fuzzy propositions—the fuzzy data—are supplied by system users. The rules are formulated in natural language reflecting whatever level of imprecision or vagueness is appropriate to the actual state of the expert's knowledge. Similarly, the fuzzy propositions mirror the degree to which the user's knowledge of the state of the world varies from vague to precise. The system combines the expert's rules with the user's knowledge of the current environment to deduce suggested decisions for the user. The system is an adviser. We ask it questions and it gives us advice. The computer doesn't need a vast amount of knowledge. We do not have to put in an encyclopedia to build a knowledge system that knows a lot about finance.

An advisory system is an expert system. The problem with expert systems is that while they can represent perhaps a large percentage of human expert knowledge, the missing percent can contain the real expertise.

The advisory system interacts intelligently with the user because it understands English. The advantage of a system that understands English is that we can ask any question we want. It does not matter if there are only a few basic ideas in the system as long as we can say whatever we want to get those ideas out. We say that advisory systems have artificial intelligence because they understand the questions we ask and make inferences to give us intelligent answers. They can have a dialogue with the user—an intelligent dialogue.

Consider the following scenario. A manager wants to balance the conflicting profit and market share goals of a company. That manager has only one explicit decision variable, PRICE. To refer to the *upcoming* decision period, the manager says NEWPRICE (Whalen and Schott, 1981).

Now, imagine that the advisory system contains the following piece of knowledge obtained from a human expert.

IF SHARE IS LOW TO MEDIUM
THEN NEWPRICE SHOULD BE BELOW OTHERS' NEWPRICE

Suppose the manager comes up with the following fuzzy propositions

MY SHARE IS LOW LOWER MEDIUM
OTHERS' NEWPRICE IS NOT TOO HIGH
Which NEWPRICE is coming?

The advisory system combines the expert rule with the user's knowledge of the current environment to *deduce* a decision for the user to evaluate.

NEWPRICE SHOULD BE LOW TO MEDIUM

The manager evaluates the advice of the system and may take some action in the environment as a result.

The advisory system makes use of APL functions and variables, both of which can be represented by English words. The default conditions of APL syntax allow a number of functions and variables to be combined into sentences whose English and APL interpretations are perfectly compatible. Thus, all production rules and fuzzy propositions existing in the advisory system or introduced by the manager correspond to well-formed APL statements. The fact that APL is interpreted rather than compiled makes it easy to add or modify individual production rules and see the result almost immediately.

An advisory system based on production rules has a high degree of clarity and naturalness at the level of individual steps. It can produce an execution trace that makes sense to anyone knowledgeable in the subject matter. There is no need for special training in computer science.

WHAT IS GOING ON?
QUALITATIVE ANALYSIS WITH SEMANTIC SYSTEMS

The essence of this discussion thus far is this: we can add a new dimension to a production system by coupling it with a semantic system. It becomes an *algorithm*. Moreover, if the semantic system is defined in an APL workspace, the production system (with minor modifications) is in itself an APL program that does calculations automatically.

A *semantic system* is a rich vocabulary. Each word in the vocabulary is defined appropriately as a constant or a simple APL function, bearing the word as its name. Thus far, we have explored semantic systems that vary with the field. In other words, the fuzzy subsets are defined on a universe of discourse, and for every field these universes are different.

A question suggests itself at this point: Can one build an independent semantic system, ready to be used by a multitude of users no matter how they formulate their questions? The answer is yes if the semantic and production systems are clearly separate. The knowledge system provides a solution to the problem of handling multiple simultaneous hypotheses and a method for ranking hypotheses in a context-sensitive way.

Of major significance is the fact that the semantic system does not evolve from a domain-specific knowledge system, but is conceived from the beginning as a domain-independent component of the knowledge system. Its development as part of a knowledge system provides a suitable framework for pursuing basic research questions in knowledge engineering.

So far we have defined fuzzy subsets as tables, number arrays, or vectors that *specify* the elements both in the domain and in the codomain. Another way to define a fuzzy subset is as a function that *generates* the tables, number arrays, or vectors or as a function with some parameters that *creates* number arrays, vectors, or tables.* For instance, a membership function may be entered as a series of numbers. That series can contain a number of discrete values, and that number can be variable. The system places the values equidistantly along the domain and then interpolates among the given values. The same technique can be used to create different shapes according to some parameters.

The problem is simplified considerably when the fuzzy subsets are defined on psychological continua. In view of this fact, we can assume that the semantic content of each word in the vocabulary is independent of context. In this case, the value of a fuzzy variable is represented by a vector. Each dimension corresponds to a point on a discrete continuum. The 11-dimensional format is most frequently used because of its association with deciles, the points ranging from 0 percent to 100 percent in increments of 10 percent. Examples of such representations appear in Chapter Four, in the section "Production Rules Can Be Derived from Verbal Models." Five primary terms LOW, HIGH, MEDIUM, UNKNOWN, and UNDEFINED can be the basis of a multitude of other linguistic values generated and used in the system.

Sometimes a crisp value is available for a particular fuzzy variable. If the crisp value happens to equal one of the discrete points on the continuum, the representation is a vector with a 1 in the corresponding dimension and 0s elsewhere. However, an APL function can use linear interpolation to compute an approximation for intermediate values, as shown below:

8	0	0	0	0	1	0	0	0	0	0	0
9	0	0	0	0	1	1	0	0	0	0	0
9.25	0	0	0	0	$\frac{1}{3}$	1	0	0	0	0	0
PRICE	0	2	4	6	8	10	12	14	16	18	20

A semantic system is a language, that is, a medium for dialogue with the computer. The versatility of the semantic system relates directly to the size of the vocabulary and the syntactical freedom it affords. Wenstop (1975) gives an example of a vocabulary.

---

* The third way to define fuzzy subsets—starting from generalized sets—is discussed in Chapter Two.

Category	Symbol	Category members
Primary terms	*T*	HIGH, LOW, MEDIUM, UNDE-FINED, UNKNOWN
Hedges	*H*	ABOVE, BELOW, AROUND UPPER, LOWER, RATHER, MORE OR LESS, VERY, NOT, NEITHER, POSSIBLY, TRULY, INDEED, FUZZILY
Connectives	*C*	AND, OR, PLUS, MINUS, TO, EXCEPT
Trend mode	*M*	INCREASINGLY, LINEARLY
Trend direction	*D*	FALLING, CLIMBING
Relation connective	R_c	THEN
Truth evaluator	IS	SHOULD BE
Pointer	*W*	WITH
Conditionalizer	IF	IF
Variable	*X*	no restriction
Value	*V*	
Relation	*R*	

Rules of syntax are used to combine vocabulary into fuzzy propositions and production rules. Four rewriting rules can define an assignment, as follows:

X	*V*		*R*	$(RR_c R)$, *D*
V	*T*, (*HV*), (*VCV*), (*RWX*)		*D*	(*HD*), (*MD*)

This means that any linguistic value, *V*, can be substituted for any compound symbol. A linguistic or fuzzy proposition has one of the following two syntactical forms:

$$X_1 \text{ IS } H\, X_2$$
$$X_1 \text{ IS } H\, V$$

For instance:

PRICE IS BELOW OTHERS' PRICE

NEWPRICE SHOULD BE EQUAL TO MEDIUM

It is easy to show that the following assignment statements are grammatical:

$Y \leftarrow$ NEITHER HIGH NOR BELOW MEDIUM
$X \leftarrow$ BELOW Y
$X \leftarrow$ AROUND Y IF Y IS NOT HIGH
$X \leftarrow X$ PLUS DX
$X \leftarrow$ HIGH IF Y IS LOW OR MEDIUM IF Y IS Z

Such a semantic system can simulate a *verbal model*—a list of linguistic assignment statements so ordered that all independent variables in a given statement have been assigned values in statements preceding it.

If we are given a verbal model, it is usually not easy to predict its behavior intuitively. This is especially true when feedback loops are used because these are difficult for the human mind to assimilate readily. What we need, therefore, is a knowledge system that understands the meaning behind assignment statements in the sense that it can make intuitively acceptable inferences from them, even when statements are not explicitly mentioned. In addition, the system must be able to put statements and inferences together and thereby calculate the *implied dynamic behavior* of the total system. In such a case, we say that the semantic system *amplifies* the knowledge of a human expert whose knowledge is a verbal model.

An expert system of this type has only two components: a semantic base and an inference procedure. The semantic base contains the meanings of the words allowed as linguistic values; the inference procedure consists of the processes that work on the verbal model specified as an input to the knowledge system, more exactly, as well-formed APL statements.

Suppose, for example, that a user wants to understand what is going on in a structure of causal relations having the following verbal model:

Use is enforced after a delay of two periods if the tension is high.

Use decreases slightly if the tension is low.

Knowledge corresponds to the current use.

Tension corresponds to visibility after a delay of one period.

Difference corresponds to knowledge if tension is not low.

Supervision increases if the difference is low.

Supervision is sustained if the current difference is not satisfactory.

Supervision decreases only if the difference is satisfactory.

Visibility relates inversely to use if supervision is low.

Otherwise, visibility is proportional to supervision.

Visibility is mitigated by increased use.

The user, after examining the vocabulary, may write the following statements.

$$U \leftarrow \text{use}$$
$$K \leftarrow \text{knowledge}$$
$$L \leftarrow \text{tension}$$
$$D \leftarrow \text{difference}$$
$$C \leftarrow \text{supervision}$$
$$V \leftarrow \text{visibility}$$

$U_t \leftarrow$ somewhat higher than U_{t-1} if L_{t-2} is very high or rather high or equal to U_{t-1} if L_{t-2} is not low or very high or slightly lower than U_{t-1} if L_{t-2} is low or rather low

$K_t \leftarrow$ very similar to U_t

$L_t \leftarrow$ very similar to V_{t-1}

$D_t \leftarrow$ similar to K_t if L_t is not low or similar to L_t if L_t is low or sort of low or rather low

$C_t \leftarrow$ considerably higher than C_{t-1} if D_t is higher than D_{t-1} and D_t is high or equal to C_{t-1} if D_t is high and D_t is not higher than D_{t-1} or D_t is not high or low or slightly lower than C_{t-1} if D_t is low

$V \leftarrow$ opposite of U_t if C_t is low or rather low or very similar to C_t if C_t is not low

$V_t \leftarrow V$ if U_t is not higher than $U_{t\ 1}$ or considerably lower than V if U_t is higher than U_{t-1}

This is an APL program. The semantic model will then be activated automatically and respond with linguistic values of output variables if the input variables are specified. For instance, if the initial state values are all "sort of high," the output will be

Period 1
USE IS VERY HIGH
TENSION IS RATHER HIGH
DIFFERENCE IS VERY HIGH
SUPERVISION IS VERY HIGH

Period 2
USE IS VERY HIGH
TENSION IS (NOT HIGH) AND NOT LOW
DIFFERENCE IS AT LEAST VERY HIGH
SUPERVISION IS VERY HIGH

All the statements in the APL program can be changed on the terminal and a complex simulation study executed to get a complex answer to the complex question

WHAT IS GOING ON?

LINGUISTIC APPROXIMATION

Any semantic system can be viewed as a pair of functions. The meaning representation part is a function from the set of linguistic values to the set of fuzzy subsets. Any word can be translated into a number array or an APL function describing how to handle these arrays. The result of this handling is another number array. *Linguistic approximation* is a function from the set of fuzzy subsets to the set of linguistic values.

The problem of linguistic approximation is associating a label with a membership distribution on the basis of semantic similarity. This can be seen as a mapping from the crisp set of all fuzzy subsets onto the language accepted by the vocabulary and syntax of the semantic system.

The problem is considerably simplified if all the fuzzy subsets are defined on the same universe of discourse. This is the case when the universe of discourse is a psychological continuum. Then primary terms and hedges are combined, and a generator generates the so-called search domain.

The search procedure tries to match the fuzzy subset to be labeled with the fuzzy subsets in the search domain. For instance, consider this knowledge base:

ANN IS VERY SHORT
NANCY IS MUCH TALLER THAN ANN
GAIL IS QUITE TALL
NANCY IS NOT MUCH SHORTER THAN GAIL

By a syntactic procedure, the system finds that

NANCY IS MUCH TALLER THAN (VERY SHORT)
AND
NOT MUCH SHORTER THAN (QUITE TALL)

Because the vocabulary contains definitions for SHORT, TALL, MUCH, VERY, QUITE, TALLER THAN, SHORTER THAN, for instance

$$\text{SHORT} \leftarrow 1 \quad 1 \quad 1 \quad 1 \quad 0.8 \quad 0.4 \quad 0 \quad 0 \quad 0 \quad 0$$
$$\text{TALL} \leftarrow 0 \quad 0 \quad 0 \quad 0 \quad 0 \quad 0 \quad 0.4 \quad 0.8 \quad 1 \quad 1$$

the fuzzy proposition is translated into a vector

$$\text{FP} \leftarrow 0 \quad 0 \quad 0 \quad 0 \quad 0 \quad 0 \quad 0.29 \quad 0.87 \quad 1 \quad 1$$

and tested against appropriate vectors in the search domain for a perfect match with a more understandable label, which in this case is INDEED TALL.

It is inefficient to perform pairwise comparisons of all the propositions allowed by the syntax of a semantic system to arrive at a linguistic approximation. One solution to this problem exploits pattern-recognition techniques. The space of membership distributions is mapped onto a feature space by evaluating some correlated features of each vector. This step is crucial because the correct selection of features determines the success or failure of almost any pattern-recognition process. A search in the low-order pattern space is performed based on a measure of semantic similarity.

A second possible solution to the problem is to exploit truth qualification. For instance we can say

IT IS VERY TRUE THAT NANCY IS TALL

This can be written more formally as

NANCY IS TALL IS VERY TRUE

where VERY TRUE is the truth qualification. The strength of the linguistic approximation is expressed as a linguistic degree of confidence. This format allows considerable flexibility in approximation, and it gives us a true sense of the uncertainty associated with the underlying data. This is possible if NANCY IS INDEED TALL is semantically equivalent to NANCY IS TALL IS VERY TRUE.

SUMMARY

1. Knowledge systems are artificial intelligence software capable of giving expert advice or analyzing complex information within limited domains.

2. A knowledge system is said to be intelligent if its response could not be judged to be different from a human response.

3. To simulate intelligence, the knowledge system internalizes a knowledge base as a model of the external world.

4. A knowledge base is a collection of facts and rules describing how the facts are linked.

5. A knowledge system internalizes the facts as objects and the rules as morphisms or arrows between objects.

6. Semantic manipulation allows production rules for inferring conclusions and taking actions to be stated in a fairly straightforward IF-THEN fashion.

7. Any production rule is an arrow

$$A \to B$$

and any production system is a chain of arrows

$$A \to B$$
$$B \to C$$
$$C \to D$$
$$\ldots$$

with the associative property

$$A \to D \to \ldots$$

8. As knowledge systems become better-known and more cost effective, a great deal of effort is being spent building software tools that can speed their development. Current work in such software tools is aimed at integrating descriptive and rule-based encoding of knowledge so that the two can work together.

9. In semantic systems, the arrow defining a production rule is supplemented by two other arrows defining the meaning of the objects, according to the following commutative diagram.

$$A \longrightarrow B$$
$$\searchrow \swarrow$$
$$[0, 1]$$

10. Knowledge systems based on semantic manipulations internalize all these arrows. Again, the production rule is an arrow

$$A' \to B'$$

but now the objects are in their turn arrows.

$$A':A \to [0,1]$$
$$B':B \to [0,1]$$

11. By defining a production rule as an arrow between objects that are arrows, we move from the category of sets to the category of arrows.

12. Changing the category means changing the logic of classifying subobjects.

13. Approximate reasoning is an inference procedure based on the logic of evaluations, which is the logic of fuzzy sets.

14. Knowledge diagrams are constructions in the category of fuzzy sets viewed as equivalent with the category of concepts (facts).

15. Any arrowless diagram

$$A \quad B$$

can be characterized with arrows. Their product is a new object C and a pair of arrows, making

$$A \leftarrow A \times B \rightarrow B$$

commute. This is a cone

$$
\begin{array}{c}
C \\
\swarrow \quad \searrow \\
A \qquad B
\end{array}
$$

as in the case of REVEAL (Chapter Six) where A, B are policy routines.

16. Any diagram

$$A \rightarrow B$$

has a cone

$$
\begin{array}{c}
C \\
\swarrow \quad \searrow \\
A \rightarrow B
\end{array}
$$

as in the case of advisory systems.

17. Consider the propositions

$$\text{IF } x \text{ is } A \text{ THEN } y \text{ is } B$$
$$x \text{ is } A^*$$

They can be represented as

$$A \rightarrow B$$
$$A^*$$

with the cones

This is the syllogism

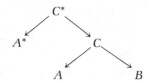

READINGS

Bonczek, B., Holsapple, C., and Whinston, A. 1981. *Foundations of decision support systems.* New York: Academic Press.

This book explores the applicability of techniques of computer science, artificial intelligence, and data base management to decision making in organizations. Both individual and collective decision makers, that is, both managers and managerial systems, are essentially information processors. In this respect, there is a bond between decision makers and computers. There are, however, clear differences in the nature and capabilities of human versus computerized information processing. The primary focus is on the extent to which the bond can be enhanced.

Of particular interest is the computerized support of relatively unstructured, nonprogrammed decision activities, such as strategic planning. The information-processing bond between decision makers and computers is strengthened by increasing the computer's ability to recognize and carry out requests while at the same time decreasing the decision maker's effort in specifying these requests. Although most expert systems were not developed with business applications in mind, such systems fit the generic pattern of decision support.

Kickert, W. 1978. *Fuzzy theories on decision making.* Leiden, Netherlands, and Boston: Martinus Nijhoff.

This book, an attempt to place the subject in historical perspective, is in two parts and seven chapters: individual decision making, decision making under constraints, multiperson decision making, multicriteria decision making, dynamic programming, dynamic systems, and linguistic modeling.

Tong, R., and Bonissone, P. 1980. A linguistic approach to decision making with fuzzy sets. *IEEE Transactions on Systems, Man, and Cybernetics* SMC-10: 716–23.

This article presents a technique for making linguistic decisions. Because fuzzy sets are an appropriate way to deal with uncertainty, decisions made on the basis of such information must also be fuzzy. To develop a technique that generates linguistic decisions, one has to draw heavily on the notions of linguistic approximation, pattern recognition, and fuzzy numbers. Tong and Bonissone discuss multichoice decision problems in which information about the *suitability* of the alternatives is given by a set of fuzzy sets. A single fuzzy set can aggregate all the suitability information; this set may be interpreted as the basic fuzzy decision. The central idea is that the preference of one alternative over the others can be expressed as a truth-qualified proposition in natural language.

Whalen, T., and Schott, B. 1981. Fuzzy production systems for decision support. *Proceedings of the International Conference on Cybernetics and Society* 649–53.

A prototype decision support system that employs fuzzy logic, production systems, and quasinatural language is described. The system includes a collection of decision rules obtained from a human expert; system users supply the fuzzy data. The rules are formulated in natural language at whatever level of precision or vagueness is appropriate to the actual state of the expert's knowledge. Similarly, the fuzzy data base mirrors the degree to which the user's knowledge of the current state of the world varies from vague to precise. The system combines the expert's rules with the user's knowledge of the current environment to deduce suggested decisions for the user to evaluate. These suggestions are presented in natural language. The primary role of the computer is as an intelligent scratchpad that keeps track of more chunks of information than human short-term memory can accommodate while imposing the fewest possible restrictions and distortions on the way the knowledge is represented. The intrinsic lattice structure that underlies fuzzy mathematics makes it easy to support ordinal- or even interval-scale data in a fuzzy production system, as well as nominal or qualitative values. In addition, the concept "close" is readily defined. If the data come close to matching the left side of a particular rule without matching it completely, then the outcome of the rule is somewhat less definite than it would have been had the match been better.

Wenstop, F. 1976. Fuzzy set simulation models in a systems dynamics perspective. *Kybernetes* 6: 290–98.

Wenstop explores the idea that an organization has to be understood as a dynamic system in which human behavior plays an important role. He introduces verbal models and discusses how to derive the consequences of their implicitly stated dynamic behavior. An efficient way to derive consequences is to postulate a semantic model based on fuzzy set theory and apply the principle of fuzzy compositional inference. If this is done, the verbal model becomes deductive when it is coupled with the semantic model, and a verbal simulation model results. If the semantic model is imposed, any verbal assignment statement is also an algorithm that (on an APL terminal) automatically computes the appropriate values of linguistic variables. The resulting values are fuzzy sets. To achieve linguistic approximation, an APL function that labels fuzzy sets with appropriate linguistic values has been implemented. This process is a heuristic search routine that develops a label by building it up stepwise from simpler elements by disjunction. The fitness criterion is the sum of the least squares.

Verbal models are powerful as pedagogical instruments by which to understand organizations informally. If we are given an APL statement, we can use interactive simulation to analyze the consequences of organizational behavior. Because this process takes place at the informal verbal level, unexpected findings might have significant implications.

Ernst, C. J. 1982. An approach to management expert systems using fuzzy logic. In *Fuzzy sets and possibility theory*, ed. R. Yager. New York: Pergamon Press.

Ernst shows the potential utility of fuzzy logic to enforce semantics and pragmatics of expert systems. He justifies this approach particularly in business consulting systems whose features must meet specific user constraints. An expert system is defined as a specialized information retrieval system with (1) a nontrivial inferential capability to understand knowledge, (2) the capability to determine the credibility of the answers given to users, and (3) the capability to explain these answers.

The reason firms need expert systems to support decision making is expressed by two words: coordination and control. Firms face coordination problems each time several decision makers share resources or participate in activities oriented toward the same goal. The complexity of a decision structure depends on two things: the size of the data base and the frequency of interactions among decision makers. A large data base implies the need for a more or less sophisticated data base management system. The frequency of interactions among decision makers increases when they have only partial knowledge of the global problem they participate in solving. From this point of view, the knowledge base of an expert system plays the role of a coordination device that expresses integrity constraints on decision making. Complexity alone, however, does not justify the use of expert systems—delay constraints must exist also. During a control process, decision makers need an interactive, on-line device to explore the space of possible actions consistent with the current state of the data base and the decision integrity constraints expressed in the knowledge base.

Rinks, D. 1982. A heuristic approach to aggregate production scheduling using linguistic variables: methodology and application. In *Fuzzy sets and possibility theory*, ed. R. Yager. New York: Pergamon Press.

Rinks illustrates how managers using simple heuristics can closely approximate the results of powerful optimizing techniques for aggregate planning and scheduling problems. Linguistic variables are used to transform reasonable rules into an operational model. This approach is possibilistic. More details about possibilistic versus probabilistic approaches can be found in Shackle, below.

Shackle, G. L. S. 1970. *Expectation, enterprise and profit: the theory of the firm.* Chicago: Aldine.

Shackle warns against the great temptation to confuse risk and uncertainty and to take a probabilistic approach to solving the problems of vagueness. Doubt about the exactness of concepts, correctness of statements and judgments, degrees of credibility and belief, and so on have little to do with probability of occurrence, the fundamental concept of the probabilistic framework.

In statistical probability, if some operation is performed repeatedly and if the possible results of this operation are exhaustively divided under a fixed list of headings, we may be able to approximate what proportion of the total number of performances have results that fall under this or that heading. The meaning and the character of this scheme need to be considered carefully. Each probability is evidently a proper fraction, and these proper fractions must evidently add up to 1. In other words, probability is a distributional value—it distributes all of the occurrences over headings.

There are two ways to arrive at such probabilities. One is by performing the operations repeatedly. The other is by discerning in the system to which the operation applies a symmetry such that no one heading has greater power to gather results than any other. In business situations, it is scarcely conceivable that a symmetry comparable to the configuration of a die could be discerned. Thus, probabilities can be discovered only by repeated trials in a long series of similar situations. Business does furnish some such possibilities. Insurance rests on this principle; so does quality control in long production runs of standardized objects.

But when a proposed experiment embodies novelty, how can one calculate a probability? How can probability have meaning for a crucial experiment, one whose repetition is logically impossible because its very performance destroys forever the conditions under which it was undertaken? The decision maker needs a scheme quite different from averaging the things that have happened to others. Probability seems an inappropriate way to evaluate a hypothesis to be tested with a nondivisible experiment.

If the method of counting cases does not apply, may it not still be legitimate to use probability to express judgments? Statisticians say yes. A vast amount of statistical literature deals with precisely this problem within the framework of probability, statistical inference, and decision. We must get in touch with the decision maker's practical frame of thought to see if the statistician's answer is correct.

The decision maker is surely concerned not with what will happen but with what can happen. The starting point for constructing a nondistributional uncertainty variable is the requirement that the measure assigned to any hypothesis shall be independent of those assigned to any and all rival hypotheses. *Possibility* is distinguished from probability by being an expression of the absence of imagined, subjective, impediments in the mind of the person who forms expectations. In this sense, *expectation* means a specific gain or loss associated with a given degree of possibility. A similar point of view can be found in Georgescu-Roegen, below.

Georgescu-Roegen, N. 1971. *The entropy law and the economic process.* Cambridge, Mass.: Harvard University Press.

This is an excellent discussion of probability, risk, and uncertainty. Risk describes situations with unknown but not novel outcomes. Uncertainty applies to cases whose outcomes we cannot predict because the same event has never occurred in the past and may thus involve novelty. Georgescu-Roegen defends the claim that the undeniably difficult problem of describing qualitative change stems from the arithmomorphic schematization.

The antinomy between "one" and "many" with which Plato, in particular, struggled is well-known. One of its roots is that the quality of discrete distinction does not necessarily pass from the arithmomorphic concept to its concrete denotations. In some cases, the transfer operates. Four pencils are an even number of pencils. A concrete triangle is a triangle, not a square. Nor is there any great difficulty in deciding that *Louis XIV* is the denotation of a king. But we can never be absolutely sure whether a concrete quadrangle is a square. In the world of ideas, "square" is "one," but in the world of the senses, it is "many." On the other hand, if we debate endlessly whether a particular country is a "democracy," it is above all because the concept itself appears as "many"; that is, it is not discretely distinct.

A vast number of concepts belong to this category. Among them are the most vital concepts in human judgments, such as "good." They have no arithmomorphic boundaries. Instead, they are surrounded by a penumbra within which they overlap with their opposites. At a particular moment in history, a nation may be both a democracy and a nondemocracy, just as there is an age when a man is both young and old. We cannot apply the fundamental law of classical logic—the principle of contradiction, "B cannot be both A and non-A"—to the category of concepts. On the contrary, we must accept that in certain cases "B is both A and non-A."

Because the principle of contradiction is a cornerstone in dialectics, Georgescu-Roegen refers to concepts that violate the principle as dialectical. Though not discretely distinct, dialectical concepts are nevertheless distinct. A penumbra separates a dialectical concept from its opposite. The separating penumbra is itself a dialectical concept.

Like all inventions, the arithmomorphic concept has its good and bad features. Although it has advanced knowledge in the domain of inert matter, it explains no process of change. Human propensities, which are the main vehicle of economic change, are not arithmomorphic concepts. The obvious conclusion is that if economics is to be a science not only of observable quantities but also of humans, it must rely extensively on dialectical reasoning, which cannot be exact. Georgescu-Roegen quotes Whitehead when he warns that as soon as one leaves the beaten track of vague clarity, one meets difficulties. Recent results confirm the need for this warning. See, for instance, Freksa, below.

Freksa, C. 1982. Linguistic description of human judgments in expert systems and in the soft sciences. In *Approximate reasoning in decision analysis*, eds. M. Gupta and E. Sanchez. Amsterdam: North-Holland.

Freksa presents a fuzzy linguistic tool for representing and analyzing human judgments in expert systems. Freksa points out the fundamental differences between measurements in the hard sciences and judgments that form the basis for decisions in the soft sciences and explains why a representation that preserves fuzziness not only is more natural but also yields more reliable results in human systems. Learning algorithms for interactive meaning adaptation of linguistic descriptors are developed by example. In conjunction with a classification program, these algorithms will be helpful for custom tailoring individual descriptor languages for specific contexts. With the aid of these algorithms, different observers will no longer need to use the same vocabulary for their descriptions. A system capable of learning the meaning of linguistic descriptors of concepts is described in Aguilar Martín and Lopez de Mantaras, below.

Aguilar Martín, J., and Lopez de Mantaras, R. 1982. The process of classification and learning the meaning of linguistic descriptors of concepts. In *Approximate reasoning in decision analysis*, eds. M. Gupta and E. Sanchez. Amsterdam: North-Holland.

Sentences in natural language are translated into PRUF. Learning consists of the adaptation of possibility distributions.

APPENDIX

The Categorial Analysis of Logic

The purpose of this appendix is to introduce the reader to the notion of a generalized set and to explain its implications for logic.

The study of generalized sets arises within category theory. A *category* can be conceived as a universe of mathematical discourse. Such a universe is determined by specifying a certain kind of object and a certain kind of transformation or morphism between objects.

The most general universe of current mathematical discourse is the category known as SET, whose objects are sets, A, B, and whose morphisms are set functions, $f:A \rightarrow B$.

The basic set-theoretic operations can be described by reference to the functions in SET. These descriptions can further be interpreted in *topoi*, categories whose structure is sufficiently like that of SET.

For instance, the category of functions $\text{SET}^{\rightarrow}$ has as objects the set functions $f:A \rightarrow B$. A morphism in $\text{SET}^{\rightarrow}$ from the object $f:A \rightarrow B$ to the object $g:C \rightarrow D$ is a pair of functions (h, k) such that

commutes; that is, $g \circ h = k \circ f$.

When we restrict attention to morphisms with a fixed codomain, we find a specialization of $\text{SET}^{\rightarrow}$. Thus, if R is the set of real numbers, we obtain the category $\text{SET} \downarrow R$ of real valued functions. The objects are all functions $f:A \to R$ that have codomain R. A morphism from $f:A \to R$ to $g:B \to R$ is a function $k:A \to B$ that makes the triangle

commute; that is, $g \circ k = f$.

In any systematic development of set theory, one of the first topics to be examined is the so-called algebra of classes. This algebra is concerned with ways of defining new sets and, when relativized to the subsets of a given set U, focuses on the operations of

$$\text{intersection: } A \cap B = \{x : x \in A \text{ and } x \in B\}$$
$$\text{union: } A \cup B = \{x : x \in A \text{ or } x \in B\}$$
$$\text{complement: } -A = \{x : x \in U \text{ and not } x \in A\}$$

The power set $P(U)$ together with the operations $\cap$, $\cup$, $-$ exhibit the structure of a *Boolean algebra*.

The classical rules of logic are represented in SET by operations on the set $\{0, 1\}$. This observation leads us to a morphism-only definition of the truth functions. For instance, *negation*

$$\neg : \{0, 1\} \to \{0, 1\}$$

is the characteristic function of the set

$$\{x : \neg x = 1\} = \{0\} \subset \{0, 1\}$$

If the inclusion function $\{0\} \subset \{0, 1\}$ is called *false*, in SET we have the following pullback.

$$
\begin{array}{ccc}
\{0\} & \xrightarrow{\ \ false\ \ } & \{0, 1\} \\
\downarrow & & \downarrow {\scriptstyle \neg} \\
\{0\} & \xrightarrow[\ \ true\ \ ]{} & \{0, 1\}
\end{array}
$$

The *conjunction*

$$\cap : \{0, 1\} \times \{0, 1\} \to \{0, 1\}$$

is the characteristic function of $< \{0\}, \{0\}>$ because the only input to

$$\{0, 1\} \times \{0, 1\} \to \{0, 1\}$$

that gives {0} is <{0},{0}>. This, being a one-element set, can be identified with a morphism

$$\{0\} \rightarrow \{0, 1\} \times \{0, 1\}$$

This morphism is the product map <true, true> that takes 0 to <true(0),
true(0)>, and hence we have the following pullback:

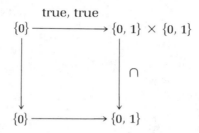

In set theory, the power set $P(U)$ is often denoted $\{0, 1\}^U$. The latter
symbol denotes the collection of all functions from U to $\{0, 1\}$. This
correspondence between subset and characteristic function can be
captured by a pullback diagram

where $\{0, 1\}$ is the classifier of the subset A.

In SET$^\rightarrow$, if $f{:}A \rightarrow B$ is a subobject of $g{:}C \rightarrow D$, then there is a commutative set diagram.

$$
\begin{array}{ccc}
A & \hookrightarrow & C \\
f \downarrow & & \downarrow g \\
B & \hookrightarrow & D
\end{array}
$$

An element x of C can be classified in three ways:

1. $x \in A$
2. $x \notin A$ but $g(x) \in B$
3. $x \in A$ and $g(x) \notin B$

We have to introduce a three-element set $\{0, \frac{1}{2}, 1\}$ to classify the subobject.

We can generalize the category SET$^\rightarrow$ to the category SET^N of *sets-
through-time*, which are objects thought of as a string

$$A \rightarrow B \rightarrow C \rightarrow$$

In this case, the classifier is the set

$$W = \{0,1,2,\ldots\}$$

W denotes the subobject classifier. Exactly as in SET, we can define truth morphisms in any topos.

$$\neg : W \to W$$
$$\cap : W \times W \to W$$
$$\cup : W \times W \to W$$

The operations $\neg$, $\cap$, $\cup$ yield an algebra of subobjects, but this algebra does not satisfy the laws of Boolean algebras, indicating that the logic of the topos is not the same as classical logic. The proper perspective is that the algebra of subobjects is non-Boolean because topos logic is nonclassical.

The principles of classical logic are represented in SET by operations on a certain set, the two-element Boolean algebra. Each topos has an analog of this algebra, and so one can say that each topos has its own logical calculus.

BIBLIOGRAPHY

Adamo, J. M. 1978. Application of fuzzy logic to the design of a behavioral model in an industrial environment. In *Current topics in cybernetics and systems*, ed. J. Rose. Berlin: Springer Verlag.

Adamo, J. M. 1978. Implementation de la théorie des sous-ensembles floues: application a l'analyse de processus de décision. Ph.D. thesis. Université Claude-Bernard, Lyons, France.

Adamo, J. M. 1980. LPL: a fuzzy programming language. *Fuzzy Sets and Systems* 3:151–79 and 261–89.

Adamo, J. M. 1981. Some applications of the LPL language to combinatorial programming. *Fuzzy Sets and Systems* 6:43–60.

Adams, E. W., and Levine, H. P. 1975. On the uncertainties transmitted from premises to conclusions in deductive inferences. *Synthese* 30:429–60.

Adlassnig, K. P. 1982. A survey on medical diagnosis and fuzzy subsets. *Approximate reasoning in decision analysis*, eds. M. Gupta and E. Sanchez. Amsterdam: North-Holland.

Adlassnig, K. P., and Kolarz, G. 1982. CADIAG-2: computer assisted medical diagnosis using fuzzy subsets. In *Approximate reasoning in decision analysis*, eds. M. Gupta and E. Sanchez. Amsterdam: North-Holland.

Aguilar Martin, J., and Lopez de Mantaras, R. 1982. The process of classification and learning the meaning of linguistic descriptors of concepts. In *Approximate reasoning in decision analysis*, eds. M. Gupta and E. Sanchez. Amsterdam: North-Holland.

Albert, P. 1978. The algebra of fuzzy logic. *Fuzzy Sets and Systems* 1:203–30.

Alston, W. 1967. Vagueness. In *Encyclopedia of philosophy*, ed. P. Edwards. New York: Macmillan.

Arbib, M. A., and Manes, E. G. 1975. A category-theoretic approach to systems in a fuzzy world. *Synthese* 30:381–406.

Baas, S. J., and Kwakernaak, H. 1977. Rating and ranking of multiple-aspect alternatives using fuzzy sets. *Automatica* 13:47–58.

Bainbridge, L. 1981. Verbal reports as evidence of the process operator's knowledge. In *Fuzzy reasoning and its applications*, eds. E. Mamdani and B. Gaines. London: Academic Press.

Baldwin, J. F. 1979. Fuzzy logic and its application to fuzzy reasoning. In *Advances in fuzzy set theory and applications*, eds. M. Gupta, R. Ragade, and R. Yager. Amsterdam: North-Holland.

Baldwin, J. F. 1979. A new approach to approximate reasoning using a fuzzy logic. *Fuzzy Sets and Systems* 2:309–25.

Baldwin, J. F. 1981. Fuzzy logic and fuzzy reasoning. In *Fuzzy reasoning and its applications*, eds. E. Mamdani and B. Gaines. London: Academic Press.

Baldwin, J. F. 1982. An automated fuzzy knowledge base. In *Fuzzy set and possibility theory*, ed. R. Yager. New York: Pergamon Press.

Baldwin, J. F., and Guild, N. C. 1980. Feasibility algorithms for approximate reasoning using a fuzzy logic. *Fuzzy Sets and Systems* 3:225–51.

Baldwin, J. F. and Pilsworth, B. 1980. An axiomatic approach to implication for approximate reasoning using fuzzy logic. *Fuzzy Sets and Systems* 3:193–219.

Bandler, W. 1983. The furtherance of possibility theory. *Human Systems Management* 3:255.

Bandler, W. and Kohout, L. J. 1981. Semantics of implication operators and fuzzy relational products. In *Fuzzy reasoning and its applications*, eds. E. Mamdani and B. Gaines. London: Academic Press.

Bandler, W., and Kohout, L. J. 1983. Probabilistic versus fuzzy production rules in expert systems. *Busefal* Printemps: 105–14.

Bellman, R. E., and Giertz, M. 1973. On the analytic formalism of the theory of fuzzy sets. *Information Sciences* 5:149–56.

Bellman, R. E., and Zadeh, L. A. 1970. Decision making in a fuzzy environment. *Management Science* 17:141–64.

Bellman, R. E., and Zadeh, L. A. 1977. Local and fuzzy logics. In *Modern uses of multiple-valued logic*, eds. J. Dunn and G. Epstein. Dordrecht, Netherlands: Reidel.

Bernard, N. 1981. Contribution à la récherche d'une théorie des ensembles flous: les multiensembles. Ph.D. thesis. Université Claude-Bernard, Lyons, France.

Black, M. 1970. *Margins of precision: essays in logic of language*. Ithaca, N.Y.: Cornell University Press.

Blanchard, N. 1982. Fuzzy-lip functions: the fuzzy-lip category. In *Fuzzy set and possibility theory*, ed. R. Yager. London: Pergamon Press.

Blockley, D. 1982. Fuzzy systems in civil engineering. In *Approximate reasoning in decision analysis*, eds. M. Gupta and E. Sanchez. Amsterdam: North-Holland.

Bonissone, P. 1979. The problem of linguistic approximation in system analysis. Ph.D. Thesis. University of California, Berkeley.

Bonissone, P. 1982. A fuzzy sets based linguistic approach: theory and applications. In *Approximate reasoning in decision analysis*, eds. M. Gupta and E. Sanchez. Amsterdam: North-Holland.

Borisov, A., and Krumberg, O. 1983. A theory of possibility for decision making. *Fuzzy Sets and Systems* 9:13–24.

Botta, O., and Delorme, M. 1982. A f-sets universe V. In *Fuzzy information and decision processes*, eds. M. Gupta and E. Sanchez. Amsterdam: North-Holland.

Buckles, B. P., and Petry, F. E. 1982. Fuzzy databases and their applications. In *Fuzzy information and decision processes*, eds. M. Gupta and E. Sanchez. Amsterdam: North-Holland.

Buckles, B. P., and Petry, F. E. 1983. Information-theoretical characterization of fuzzy relational data bases. *IEEE Trans. Systems, Man, and Cybernetics* SMC-13:74–77.

Carrega, J. C. 1983. The categories Set*H* and Fuz*H*. *Fuzzy Sets and Systems* 9:327–32.

Cayrol, M., Farreny, H., and Prade, H. 1982. Fuzzy pattern matching. *Kybernetes* 11:103–16.

Cerruti, U. 1981. A categorial point of view in fuzzy theories. *Proceedings of the Third International Seminar on Fuzzy Set Theory*, Institut für Mathematik, Johannes Kepler Universität, Linz, Austria.

Chakraborty, M., and Das, M. 1983. Studies in fuzzy relations over fuzzy subsets. *Fuzzy Sets and Systems* 9:79–90.

Chanas, S., and Kolodziejczyk, W. 1982. Maximum flow in a network with fuzzy arc capacities. *Fuzzy Sets and Systems* 8: 165–73.

Czogala, E., and Pedrycz, W. 1981. On identification in fuzzy systems and its applications in control. *Fuzzy Sets and Systems* 6: 73–83.

Dempster, A. P. 1967. Upper and lower probabilities induced by a multivalued mapping. *Annals of Mathematical Statistics* 38:325–39.

Dempster, A. P. 1968. A generalization of Bayesian inference. *J. Royal Statistical Society* B-30:205–47.

Dinola, A., and Ventre, A. 1981. Criteria and linear orderings of fuzzy sets. *Kybernetes* 10:271–73.

Dinola, A., and Ventre, A. 1982. Ordering via fuzzy entropy. In *Fuzzy information and decision processes*, eds. M. Gupta and E. Sanchez. Amsterdam: North-Holland.

Dinola, A., and Ventre, A. 1982–83. Pointwise choice criteria determined by global properties. *Busefal* Hiver:89–97.

Dubois, D., and Prade, H. 1980. *Fuzzy sets and systems: theory and applications.* New York: Academic Press.

Dubois, D., and Prade, H. 1982. On several representations of an uncertain body of evidence. In *Fuzzy information and decision processes*, eds. M. Gupta and E. Sanchez. Amsterdam: North-Holland.

Dubois, D., and Prade, H. 1982. Towards the analysis and synthesis of fuzzy mappings. In *Fuzzy set and possibility theory*, ed. R. Yager. New York: Pergamon Press.

Dubois, D., and Prade, H. 1982. The use of fuzzy numbers in decision analysis. In *Fuzzy information and decision processes*, eds. M. Gupta and E. Sanchez. Amsterdam: North-Holland.

Dubois, D., and Prade, H. 1983. Using possibility theory for modeling qualitative data in human systems. *Human Systems Management* 3:265–66.

Dumitru, V., and Luban, F. 1981. Membership functions, some mathematical programming models and production scheduling. *Fuzzy Sets and Systems* 8:19–33.

Efstathiou, J., and Rajkovic, V. 1979. Multiattribute decision making using a fuzzy heuristic approach. *IEEE Trans. Systems, Man, and Cybernetics* SMC-9:326–33.

Ernst, C. J. 1981. An approach to management expert systems using fuzzy logic. In *Applied systems and cybernetics*, ed. G. Lasker. New York: Pergamon Press.

Ernst, C. J. 1982. An approach to management expert systems using fuzzy logic. In *Fuzzy sets and possibility theory*, ed. R. Yager. New York: Pergamon Press.

Ernst, C. J. 1982. Le modèle de raisonnement approché du système MANAGER. *Busefal* 9:93–99.

Eshragh, F., and Mamdani, E. H. 1981. A general approach to linguistic approximation. In *Fuzzy reasoning and its applications*, eds. E. Mamdani and B. Gaines. London: Academic Press.

Esogbue, A. O. 1983. Dynamic programming, fuzzy sets, and the models of R&D management control systems. *IEEE Trans. Systems, Man, and Cybernetics* SMC-13:18–30.

Esogbue, A. O., and Ahipo, Z. 1982. Fuzzy sets and water resources planning. In *Fuzzy set and possibility theory*, ed. R. Yager. New York: Pergamon Press.

Esogbue, A. O., and Elder, R. C. 1979 and 1980. Fuzzy sets and the modeling of physician decision processes. *Fuzzy Sets and Systems* 2(1979):279–91 and 3(1980):1–9.

Fieschi, M., Joubert, M., Fieschi, D., Soula, G., and Roux, M. 1982. SPHINX: an interactive system for medical diagnosis aids. In *Approximate reasoning in decision analysis*, eds. M. Gupta and E. Sanchez. Amsterdam: North-Holland.

Fiksel, J. 1982. Applications of fuzzy set and possibility theory to system management. In *Fuzzy set and possibility theory*, ed. R. Yager. New York: Pergamon Press.

Freksa, C. 1982. Linguistic description of human judgments in expert systems and soft sciences. In *Approximate reasoning in decision analysis*, eds. M. Gupta and E. Sanchez. Amsterdam: North-Holland.

Fu, K. S., Ishizuka, M., and Yao, J. T. P. 1982. Applications of fuzzy sets in earthquake engineering. In *Fuzzy set and possibility theory*, ed. R. Yager. New York: Pergamon Press.

Fukami, S., Mizumoto, M., and Tanaka, K. 1980. Some considerations on fuzzy conditional inference. *Fuzzy Sets and Systems* 4:243–73.

Gaines, B. R. 1977. Foundations of fuzzy reasoning. In *Fuzzy automata and decision processes*, eds. M. Gupta, G. Saridis, and B. Gaines. Amsterdam: North-Holland.

Gaines, B. R. 1982. Logical foundations of database systems. In *Approximate reasoning in decision analysis*, eds. M. Gupta and E. Sanchez. Amsterdam: North-Holland.

Georgescu, G. 1971. The theta-valued Lukasiewicz algebras. *Revue Roumaine de Mathématiques Pures et Appliquées* 16:195–209 and 1365–90.

Georgescu, G., and Vraciu, C. 1970. On the characterization of central Lukasiewicz algebras. *Journal of Algebra* 16:486–95.

Geyer, F., and van der Zouwen, J. 1982. *Dependence and inequality*. London: Pergamon Press.

Giles, R. 1980. A computer program for fuzzy reasoning. *Fuzzy Sets and Systems* 4:221–34.

Giles, R. 1981. Lukasiewicz logic and fuzzy set theory. In *Fuzzy reasoning and its applications*, eds. E. Mamdani and B. Gaines. London: Academic Press.

Giles, R. 1982. Semantics for fuzzy reasoning. *Int. J. Man-Machine Studies* 17:401–15.

Giles, R. 1983. The practical interpretation of fuzzy concepts. *Human Systems Management* 3:263–64.

Goguen, J. A. 1969. Categories of V-sets. *Bulletin of the American Mathematical Society* 75:622–24.

Goguen, J. A. 1969. The logic of inexact concepts. *Synthese* 19:325–73.

Goguen, J. A. 1979. Fuzzy sets and the social nature of truth. In *Advances in fuzzy set theory and applications*, eds. M. Gupta, R. Ragade, R. Yager. Amsterdam: North-Holland.

Goldblatt, R. 1979. *Topoi: the categorial analysis of logic.* Amsterdam: North-Holland.

Gorzalczany, M., Kiszka, J., and Stacowicz, M. 1982. Some problems of studying adequacy of fuzzy models. In *Fuzzy set and possibility theory*, ed. R. Yager. New York: Pergamon Press.

Gouvernet, J., Ayme, S., and Sanchez, E. 1982. Approximate reasoning in medical genetics. In *Fuzzy set and possibility theory*, ed. R. Yager. New York: Pergamon Press.

Haak, S. 1979. Do we need fuzzy logic? *Int. J. Man-Machine Studies* 11:437–45.

Heines, J. M. 1983. Basic concepts in knowledge-based systems. *Machine-Mediated Learning* 1:65–95.

Hersh, H. M. 1976. Fuzzy reasoning: the integration of vague information. Ph.D. thesis. The Johns Hopkins University, Baltimore.

Hersh, H. M., and Caramazza, A. 1976. A fuzzy set approach to modifiers and vagueness in natural language. *Journal of Experimental Psychology* 105:254–76.

Hipel, K. W. 1982. Fuzzy set methodologies in multicriteria modeling. In *Fuzzy information and decision processes*, eds. M. Gupta and E. Sanchez. Amsterdam: North-Holland.

Hisdal, E. 1982. A fuzzy IF-THEN-ELSE relation with guaranteed correct inference. In *Fuzzy set and possibility theory*, ed. R. Yager. New York: Pergamon Press.

Holmblad, L. P., and Ostergaard, J. J. 1982. Control of a cement kiln by fuzzy logic. In *Fuzzy information and decision processes*, eds. M. Gupta and E. Sanchez. Amsterdam: North-Holland.

Huntsberger, T. 1983. Flash: a multivalued logic based expert system for image understanding. Technical report of the Computer Vision Laboratory, Dept. of Computer Science, University of South Carolina, Columbia.

Imaoka, H., Terano, T., and Sugeno, M. 1982. Recognition of linguistically instructed path to destination. In *Approximate reasoning in decision analysis*, eds. M. Gupta and E. Sanchez. Amsterdam: North-Holland.

Ishizuka, M., Fu, K. S., and Yao, J. T. P. 1982a. Inference procedures under uncertainty for the problem-reduction method. *Information Sciences* 28:179–206.

Ishizuka, M., Fu, K. S., and Yao, J. T. P. 1982b. A rule based inference with fuzzy set for structural damage assessment. In *Approximate reasoning in decision analysis*, eds. M. Gupta and E. Sanchez. Amsterdam: North-Holland.

Jones, P. 1983. REVEAL: fuzzy sets and expert systems in corporate modeling. Communication at the 2d Annual Conference of NAFIP at Schenectady, New York.

Jones, P., and Morton, P. 1982. REVEAL. In *Computer based planning systems*, eds. T. Naylor and M. Mann. Oxford, Ohio: Planning Executive Institute.

Kabbara, G. 1982. New utilization of fuzzy optimization method. In *Fuzzy information and decision processes*, eds. M. Gupta and E. Sanchez. Amsterdam: North-Holland.

Kacprzyk, J. 1983. *Multistage decision-making under fuzziness*. Cologne, Germany: Verlag TUV.

Kacprzyk, J., and Yager, R. 1982. *Emergency-oriented expert systems: a fuzzy approach*. Tech. Report MII-213/247, Machine Intelligence Institute, Iona College, New Rochelle, New York.

Kacprzyk, J., and Yager, R. 1983. Softer optimization and control model via fuzzy linguistic quantifiers. Communication at the 2d Annual Conference of NAFIP at Schenectady, New York.

Kampe de Feriet, J. 1982. Interpretation of membership function of fuzzy sets in terms of plausibility and belief. In *Fuzzy information and decision processes*, eds. M. Gupta and E. Sanchez. Amsterdam: North-Holland.

Kandel, A. 1982. *Fuzzy techniques in pattern recognition*. New York: Wiley.

Kandel, A. 1983. On possibility theory. *Human Systems Management* 3:261–62.

Kania, A. 1982. Fuzzy transformations in terms of possibilistic measure. In *Fuzzy set and possibility theory*, ed. R. Yager. New York: Pergamon Press.

Kaufmann, A. 1973, 1975, and 1977. *Introduction a la théorie des sous-ensembles flous*, 4 vols. Paris: Mason.

Kerre, E. E. 1982. The use of fuzzy set theory in electrocardiological diagnosis. In *Approximate reasoning in decision analysis*, eds. M. Gupta and E. Sanchez. Amsterdam: North-Holland.

Kickert, W. 1978. *Fuzzy theories on decision making*. Leiden, Netherlands: Martinus Nijhoff.

Kickert, W. 1979. An example of linguistic modeling: the case of Mulder's theory of power. In *Advances in fuzzy set theory and applications*, eds. M. Gupta, R. Ragade, and R. Yager. Amsterdam: North-Holland.

King, P. J., and Mamdani, E. H. 1977. The application of fuzzy control systems to industrial processes. *Automatica* 13:235–42.

Kling, R. 1974. Fuzzy-PLANNER: reasoning with inexact concepts in a procedural problem-solving language. *Journal of Cybernetics* 4:105–22.

Kochen, M. 1979. Enhancement of coping through blurring. *Fuzzy Sets and Systems* 2:37–52.

Kochen, M. 1983. Is fuzzy set theory appropriate for models of human behavior? *Human Systems Management* 3:268–69.

Kuzmin, V. 1981. A parametric approach to description of variables and hedges. *Fuzzy Sets and Systems* 6:27–42.

Kwakernaak, H. 1979. An algorithm for rating multiple-aspect alternatives using fuzzy sets. *Automatica* 15:615–16.

Lakoff, G. 1973. Hedges: a study in meaning criteria and the logic of fuzzy concepts. *Journal of Philosophical Logic* 2:458–508.

Larsen, P. M. 1981. Industrial applications of fuzzy logic control. In *Fuzzy reasoning and its applications*, eds. E. Mamdani and B. Gaines. London: Academic Press.

Lefaivre, R. 1974. Fuzzy problem solving. Ph.D. thesis, University of Wisconsin, Madison.

Lefaivre, R. 1974. The representation of fuzzy knowledge. *Journal of Cybernetics* 4:57–66.

Lesmo, L., Saitta, L., and Torasso, P. 1982. Learning of fuzzy production rules for medical diagnosis. In *Approximate reasoning and decision analysis*, eds. M. Gupta and E. Sanchez. Amsterdam: North-Holland.

Mamdani, E. H. 1977. Application of fuzzy logic to approximate reasoning using linguistic systems. *IEEE Trans. on Computers* C-26:1182–91.

Mamdani, E. H. 1977. Applications of fuzzy set theory to control systems: a survey. In *Fuzzy automata and decision processes*, eds. M. Gupta, G. Saridis, and B. Gaines. Amsterdam: North-Holland.

Manes, E. G. 1982. Book review essay: fuzzy sets and systems. *Bulletin of the American Mathematical Society* 7:603–12.

Martin-Clouaire, R., and Prade, H. 1983. On the problem of representation and propagation of uncertainty in expert systems. Communication at the 2d Annual Conference of NAFIP at Schenectady, New York.

Mizumoto, M. 1982. Fuzzy inference using max composition in the compositional rule of inference. In *Approximate reasoning in decision analysis*, eds. M. Gupta and E. Sanchez. Amsterdam: North-Holland.

Mizumoto, M., Fukami, S., and Tanaka, K. 1979. Some methods of fuzzy reasoning. In *Advances in fuzzy set theory and applications*, eds. M. Gupta, R. Ragade, and R. Yager. Amsterdam: North-Holland.

Mizumoto, M., and Zimmermann, H. J. 1982. Comparison of fuzzy reasoning methods. *Fuzzy Sets and Systems* 8:253–83.

Mukaidono, M. 1982. Fuzzy inference of resolution style. In *Fuzzy set and possibility theory*, ed. R. Yager. New York: Pergamon Press.

Natvig, B. 1983. Possibility versus probability. *Fuzzy Sets and Systems* 9:219–28.

Negoita, C. V. 1969. Information retrieval systems. Ph.D. thesis. Polytechnical Institute, Bucharest.

Negoita, C. V. 1970. *Information storage and retrieval*. Bucharest: Academy Press.

Negoita, C. V. 1979. *Management applications of system theory*. Basel, Switzerland: Birkhäuser Verlag.

Negoita, C. V. 1981. *Fuzzy systems*. Tunbridge Wells, England: Abacus Press.

Negoita, C. V. 1982. On the cybernetics of human systems. In *Dependence and inequality*, eds. R. Geyer and J. van der Zouwen. London: Pergamon Press.

Negoita, C. V., and Flondor, P. 1976. On fuzziness in information retrieval. *Int. J. Man-Machine Studies* 8:711–16.

Negoita, C. V., Flondor, P., and Sularia, M. 1977. On fuzzy environment in optimization problems. In *Modern trends in cybernetics and systems*, eds. J. Rose and C. Bilciu. Berlin: Springer Verlag.

Negoita, C. V., and Ralescu, D. A. 1974. *Fuzzy sets and their applications*. Bucharest: Technical Press.

Negoita, C. V., and Ralescu, D. A. 1975. *Applications of fuzzy sets to systems analysis*. Basel, Switzerland and Boston: Birkhäuser Verlag, and New York: Halsted Press.

Negoita, C. V., and Roman, R. 1980. On the logic of discrete systems dynamics. *Kybernetes* 9:189–92.

Negoita, C. V., and Stefanescu, A. 1975. On the state equation of fuzzy systems. *Kybernetes* 4:213–16.

Negoita, C. V., and Stefanescu, A. 1982. On fuzzy optimization. In *Fuzzy information and decision processes*, eds. M. Gupta and E. Sanchez. Amsterdam: North-Holland.

Negoita, C. V., and Sularia, M. 1976. On fuzzy mathematical programming and tolerances in planning. *Economic Computation and Economic Cybernetics Studies and Research* (published by the Academy of Economic Studies, Bucharest, Romania) 1:3–15.

Nguyen, H. T. 1978. On conditional possibility distributions. *Fuzzy Sets and Systems* 1:299–309.

Oden, G., and Lopes, L. 1982. On the internal structure of fuzzy subjective categories. In *Fuzzy set and possibility theory*, ed. R. Yager. New York: Pergamon Press.

Ogawa, H., Fu, K. S., and Yao, J. C. T. 1983. An inexact inference method using fuzzy sets. Communication at the 2d Annual Conference of NAFIP at Schenectady, New York.

Orlovsky, S. A. 1977. On programming with fuzzy constraint sets. *Kybernetes* 6:197–201.

Ovchinnikov, S. 1981. Structure of fuzzy binary relations. *Fuzzy Sets and Systems* 6:169–95.

Pedrycz, W. 1982. Some aspects of fuzzy decision making. *Kybernetes* 11:297–301.

Pitts, A. M. 1981. Fuzzy sets do not form a topos. *Fuzzy Sets and Systems* 8:101–104.

Ponasse, D. 1978. Algèbres floues at algèbres de Lukasiewicz. *Revue Roumaine de Mathématiques Pures et Appliquées* 12:103–11.

Ponasse, D. 1983. Some remarks on the category FuzH of M. Eytan. *Fuzzy Sets and Systems* 9:199–204.

Prade, H. 1982. Modal semantics and fuzzy set theory. In *Fuzzy set and possibility theory*, ed. R. Yager. New York: Pergamon Press.

Prade, H. 1982. Modèles mathématiques de l'imprécis et de l'incertain en vue d'applications au raisonnement naturel. Ph.D. thesis. Université Paul Sabatier, Toulouse, France.

Prade, H. 1983. Approximate and plausible reasoning: the state of the art. Communication at the IFAC Symposium on Fuzzy Information, Knowledge Representation, and Decision Analysis, July 1983, Marseilles.

Prade, H. 1983. Data bases with fuzzy information and approximate reasoning in expert systems. *Busefal* Printemps:115–25.

Radecki, T. 1983. A theoretical background for applying fuzzy set theory in information retrieval. *Fuzzy Sets and Systems* 10:169–83.

Ralescu, D. A. 1978. Fuzzy subobjects in a category and the theory of C-sets. *Fuzzy Sets and Systems* 1:193–202.

Ralescu, D. A. 1979. A survey of the representation of fuzzy concepts and its applications. In *Advances in fuzzy set theory and applications*, eds. M. Gupta, R. Ragade, and R. Yager. Amsterdam: North-Holland.

Rinks, D. B. 1982. The performance of fuzzy algorithmic models for aggregate planning under different cost structures. In *Fuzzy information and decision processes*, eds. M. Gupta and E. Sanchez. Amsterdam: North-Holland.

Robinson, E., and Turner, S. J. 1981. Improving library effectiveness: a proposal for applying fuzzy set concepts in the management of large collections. *Journal of the American Society for Information Science* 1981:458–62.

Rosenfeld, A. 1982. How many are a few? Fuzzy sets, fuzzy numbers, and fuzzy mathematics. *Mathematical Intelligencer* 1982.

Ruspini, E. H. 1982. Possibilistic data structures for the representation of uncertainties. In *Approximate reasoning in decision analysis*, eds. M. Gupta and E. Sanchez. Amsterdam: North-Holland.

Saaty, T. L. 1978. Exploring the interface between hierarchies, multiple objectives, and fuzzy sets. *Fuzzy Sets and Systems* 1:57–68.

Sanchez, E. 1979. Medical diagnosis based on composite fuzzy relations. In *Advances in fuzzy set theory and applications*, eds. M. Gupta, R. Ragade, and R. Yager. Amsterdam: North-Holland.

Sanchez, E. 1982. Possibility distributions, fuzzy intervals, and possibility measures in a linguistic approach to pattern classification in medicine. In *Systems concepts in medicine and clinical behavioral sciences*, eds. J. Kohout, W. Bandler, and G. Stern. New York: Elsevier.

Sanchez, E., Gouvernet, J., Bartolin, R., and Vovan, L. 1982. Linguistic approach in fuzzy logic of the WHO classification of dyslipoproteinemias. In *Fuzzy set and possibility theory*, ed. R. Yager. New York: Pergamon Press.

Schefe, P. 1981. On foundations of reasoning with uncertain facts and vague concepts. In *Fuzzy reasoning and its applications*, eds. E. Mamdani and B. Gaines. London: Academic Press.

Shafer, G. 1976. *A mathematical theory of evidence*. Princeton: Princeton University Press.

Shortliffe, E. H., and Buchanan, B. G. 1975. A model of inexact reasoning in medicine. *Mathematical Biosciences* 23:351–79.

Silvert, W. 1979. Symmetric summation: a class of operations on fuzzy sets. *IEEE Trans. Systems, Man, and Cybernetics* SMC-9:657–59.

Skala, H. J. 1982. Modelling vagueness. In *Fuzzy information and decision processes*, eds. M. Gupta and E. Sanchez. Amsterdam: North-Holland.

Soula, G., and Sanchez, E. 1982. Soft deduction rules in medical diagnosis processes. In *Approximate reasoning in decision analysis*, eds. M. Gupta and E. Sanchez. Amsterdam: North-Holland.

Sugeno, M. 1974. Theory of fuzzy integral and its applications. Ph.D. thesis. Tokyo Institute of Technology.

Sugeno, M., and Terano, T. 1975. Conditional fuzzy measures and their applications. In *Fuzzy sets and their applications to cognitive and decision processes*, eds. L. Zadeh, K. Fu, K. Tanaka, and M. Shimura. New York: Academic Press.

Sugeno, M., and Takagi, T. 1983. Multidimensional fuzzy reasoning. *Fuzzy Sets and Systems* 9:313–26.

Takeda, E. 1982. Interactive identification of fuzzy outranking relations in a multicriteria decision problem. In *Fuzzy information and decision processes*, eds. M. Gupta and E. Sanchez. Amsterdam: North-Holland.

Tanaka, H., Okuda, T., and Asai, K. 1974. On fuzzy mathematical programming. *Journal of Cybernetics* 3:37–46.

Tanaka, H., Tsukiyama, T., and Asai, K. 1982. A fuzzy system model based on logical structure. In *Fuzzy set and possibility theory*, ed. R. Yager. New York: Pergamon Press.

Tanaka, K. 1982. Resume on dealing with uncertainty/ambiguity in cojunction with knowledge engineering. In *Fuzzy set and possibility theory*, ed. R. Yager. New York: Pergamon Press.

Togai, M. 1982. Principles and applications of fuzzy inference: a new approach to decision-making processes in ill-defined systems. Ph.D. thesis. Dept. of Electrical Engineering, Duke University, Chapel Hill, N.C.

Togai, M. 1983. Analysis and control of fuzzy dynamic systems. Communication at the 2d Annual Conference of NAFIP at Schenectady, New York.

Tong, R. M. 1977. A control engineering review of fuzzy systems. *Automatica* 13: 559–69.

Tong, R. M. 1980. The evaluation of fuzzy models derived from experimental data. *Fuzzy Sets and Systems* 4:1–12.

Tong, R. M. 1983. Fuzzy sets and multicriteria decision making. *Human Systems Management* 3:226–68.

Tong, R. M., and Bonissone, P. 1980. A linguistic approach to decision making with fuzzy sets. *IEEE Trans. Systems, Man, and Cybernetics* SMC-10: 716–23.

Tong, R. M. and Efstathiou, J. 1982. A critical assessment of truth functional modification and its use in approximate reasoning. *Fuzzy Sets and Systems* 7:103–108.

Tong, R. M., Shapiro, D., McCune, B., and Dean, J. 1983. A rule-based approach to information retrieval: some results and comments. Report of Advanced Information and Decision Systems, Mountain View, Calif.

Trillas, E. 1980. *Conjuntos borrosos.* Barcelona: Vicens-Vives. (Reviewed in *Fuzzy Sets and Systems* 6(1980).

Trillas, E., Alsina, C., and Valverde, L. 1982. Do we need max, min and 1-j in fuzzy set theory? In *Fuzzy set and possibility theory,* ed. R. Yager. New York: Pergamon Press.

Tsukamoto, Y. 1979. An approach to fuzzy reasoning method. In *Advances in fuzzy set theory and applications,* eds. M. Gupta, R. Ragade, and R. Yager. Amsterdam: North-Holland.

Tsukamoto, Y. 1979. Fuzzy logic based on Lukasiewicz logic and its applications in diagnosis and control. Ph.D. thesis. Tokyo Institute of Technology.

Tsukamoto, Y. 1982. Concept of linguistic measure. *Proceedings of the Fourth International Seminar on Fuzzy Set Theory,* Institut für Mathematik, Johannes Kepler Universität, Linz, Austria.

Umano, M. 1982. FREEDOM-O: a fuzzy data base system. In *Fuzzy information and decision processes,* eds. M. Gupta and E. Sanchez. Amsterdam: North-Holland.

Umano, M., Mizumoto, M., and Tanaka, K. 1978. FSTDS—a fuzzy set manipulation system. *Information Sciences* 14:115–59.

Umbers, I. G., and King, P. J. 1981. An analysis of human decision making in cement kiln control and the implementation for automation. In *Fuzzy reasoning and its applications,* eds. E. Mamdani and B. Gaines. London: Academic Press.

Uragami, M., Mizumoto, M., and Tanaka, K. 1976. Fuzzy robot controls. *Journal of Cybernetics* 6:39–64.

Verdegay, J. L. 1982. Fuzzy mathematical programming. In *Fuzzy information and decision processes,* M. Gupta and E. Sanchez. Amsterdam: North-Holland.

Verma, R. R. 1970. Vagueness and the principle of the excluded middle. *Mind* 79:66–77.

Wang, P. P., and Chang, S. K., eds. 1980. *Fuzzy set theory and applications to policy analysis and information systems*. New York: Plenum.

Watanabe, S. 1978. On a generalized fuzzy set theory. *IEEE Trans. Systems, Man, and Cybernetics* SMC-8:756–59.

Watson, S. R., Weiss, J. J., and Donell, M. L. 1979. Fuzzy decision analysis. *IEEE Trans. Systems, Man, and Cybernetics* SMC-9:1–9.

Wechler, W. 1978. *The concept of fuzziness in automata and language theory*. Berlin: Akademic Verlag.

Wechsler, H. 1976. A fuzzy approach to medical diagnosis. *Int. J. Bio-Medical Computing* 7:191–203.

Weiss, J. J., and Donell, M. L. 1979. A general-purpose, policy-capturing device using fuzzy production rules. In *Advances in fuzzy set theory and applications*, eds. M. Gupta, R. Ragade, and R. Yager. Amsterdam: North-Holland.

Wenstop, F. 1975. Applications of linguistic variables in the analysis of organizations. Ph.D. thesis. University of California, Berkeley.

Wenstop, F. 1979. Exploring linguistic consequences of assertions in social sciences. In *Advances in fuzzy set theory and applications*, eds. M. Gupta, R. Ragade, and R. Yager. Amsterdam: North-Holland.

Whalen, T., and Schott, B. 1981. Fuzzy production systems for decision support. *Proceedings of the International Conference on Cybernetics and Society.* 649–53.

Whalen, T., and Schott, B. 1983. Alternative logics for approximate reasoning: a comparative study. Communication at the 2d Annual Conference of NAFIP at Schenectady, New York.

Whalen, T., Schott, B., and Ganoe, F. 1982. Fault diagnosis in a fuzzy network. Report of the Decision Science Laboratory, Dept. of Quantitative Methods, Georgia State University, Atlanta.

Whalster, W. 1981. Implementing fuzziness in dialogue systems. In *Empirical semantics*, ed. B. Rieger. Bochum, West Germany: Brockmeyer.

Whalster, W. 1981. *Natürlichsprachliche Argumentation in Dialogsystemen*. Berlin: Springer Verlag.

Wiedey, G., and Zimmermann, H. J. 1978. Media selection and fuzzy linear programming. *J. Operations Research Society* 29:1071–84.

Wierzshon, S. T. 1982. Applications of fuzzy decision making theory to coping with ill-defined problems. *Fuzzy Sets and Systems* 7:1–18.

Wierzshon, S. T. 1982. On fuzzy measure and fuzzy integral. In *Fuzzy information and decision processes*, eds. M. Gupta and E. Sanchez. Amsterdam: North-Holland.

Wilmott, R. 1980. Two fuzzier implication operators in the theory of fuzzy power sets. *Fuzzy Sets and Systems* 4:31–36.

Wynne, B. 1982. Qualitative modeling: a beginning. *Interfaces* 12:34–36.

Yager, R. 1978. Linguistic models and fuzzy truths. *Int. J. Man-Machine Studies* 10:483–94.

Yager, R. 1978. Validation of fuzzy linguistic models. *Journal of Cybernetics* 8:17–30.

Yager, R. 1980. An approach to inference in approximate reasoning. *Int. J. Man-Machine Studies* 13:323–38.

Yager, R. 1980. A foundation for a theory of possibility. *Journal of Cybernetics* 10:177–204.

Yager, R. 1980. On a general class of fuzzy connectives. *Fuzzy Sets and Systems* 4:235–42.

Yager, R. 1980. Some observations on probabilistic qualification in approximate reasoning. *Information Sciences* 22:217–34.

Yager, R. 1983. Hedging in the combination of evidence. *J. Information and Optimization Sciences* 4:73–81.

Yager, R. 1983. An introduction to applications of possibility theory. *Human Systems Management* 3:246–53.

Zadeh, L. A. 1968. Fuzzy algorithms. *Information and Control* 12:94–102.

Zadeh, L. A. 1972. A fuzzy set theoretic interpretation of linguistic hedges. *Journal of Cybernetics* 2:4–34.

Zadeh, L. A. 1973. Outline of a new approach to the analysis of complex systems and decision processes. *IEEE Trans. Systems, Man, and Cybernetics* SMC-3:28–44.

Zadeh, L. A. 1975. Calculus of fuzzy restrictions. In *Fuzzy sets and their applications in cognitive and decision processes*, eds. L. Zadeh, K. Fu, K. Tanaka, and M. Shimura. New York: Academic Press.

Zadeh, L. A. 1975. The concept of a linguistic variable and its application to approximate reasoning. *Information Sciences* 8:199–249 and 301–57, 9:43–80.

Zadeh, L. A. 1975. Fuzzy logic and approximate reasoning. *Synthese* 30:407–28.

Zadeh, L. A. 1976. The linguistic approach and its application to decision analysis. In *Directions in large-scale systems*, eds. Y. Ho and S. Mitter. New York: Plenum.

Zadeh, L. A. 1979. A theory of approximate reasoning. In *Machine intelligence*, vol. 9, eds. J. Hayes, D. Michie, and L. Mikulich. New York: Elsevier.

Zadeh, L. A. 1981. Test score semantics for natural languages and meaning representation via PRUF. In *Empirical semantics*, ed. B. Rieger. Bochum, West Germany: Brockmeyer.

Zadeh, L. A. 1983. Commonsense knowledge representation based on fuzzy logic. *Computer* 16:61–65..

Zadeh, L. A. 1983. Is possibility different from probability? *Human Systems Management* 3:253–54.

Zeleny, M. 1981. Fuzzy sets: precision and relevancy. In *Applied systems and cybernetics,* ed. G. Lasker. New York: Pergamon Press.

Zeleny, M. 1981. *Multiple criteria decision making.* New York: McGraw-Hill.

Zimmermann, H. J. 1975. Description and optimization of fuzzy systems. *Int. J. General Systems* 2:209–15.

Zimmermann, H. J. 1978. Fuzzy programming and linear programming with several objective functions. *Fuzzy Sets and Systems* 1:45–55.

Zimmermann, H. J., and Zysno, P. 1980. Latent connectives in human decision making. *Fuzzy Sets and Systems* 4:37–52.

INDEX